A YEAR OF THINKING DEEPLY ABOUT THE GOOD BOOK

Linda, You are a beautiful person. I sense in you an awe and reverence for God's word. What a blessing for the church to have you as a teacher. God Bless, John

JOHN ASH

CROSSBOOKS
PUBLISHING

CrossBooks™
A Division of LifeWay
1663 Liberty Drive
Bloomington, IN 47403
www.crossbooks.com
Phone: 1-866-879-0502

© 2011 John Ash. All rights reserved.

No part of this book may be reproduced, stored in a retrieval system, or transmitted by any means without the written permission of the author.

First published by CrossBooks 11/17/2011

ISBN: 978-1-4627-0689-1 (sc)
ISBN: 978-1- 4627-0692-1 (hc)
ISBN: 978-1-4627-1106-2 (e)

Printed in the United States of America

This book is printed on acid-free paper.

Certain stock imagery © Thinkstock.
Any people depicted in stock imagery provided by Thinkstock are models, and such images are being used for illustrative purposes only.

Because of the dynamic nature of the Internet, any web addresses or links contained in this book may have changed since publication and may no longer be valid. The views expressed in this work are solely those of the author and do not necessarily reflect the views of the publisher, and the publisher hereby disclaims any responsibility for them.

Contents

1st Sunday – Read Genesis 1-5 1

2nd Sunday – Read Genesis 6-36 3

3rd Sunday – Read Genesis 37-50 5

4th Sunday – Read Exodus 1-11 7

5th Sunday – Read Exodus 12-31 10

6th Sunday – Read Exodus 32-40, Leviticus 1-9 13

7th Sunday – Read Leviticus 10-27 16

8th Sunday – Read Numbers 1-10 19

9th Sunday – Read Numbers 11-36 22

10th Sunday – Read Deuteronomy 25

11th Sunday – Read Joshua 28

12th Sunday – Read Judges 31

13th Sunday – Read Ruth 34

14th Sunday – Read 1 Samuel 1-16 37

15th Sunday – Read 1 Samuel 16-31 41

16th Sunday – Read 2 Samuel 1-10 45

17th Sunday – Read 2 Samuel 11-24 49

18th Sunday – Read 1 Kings 1-11 55

19th Sunday – Read 1 Kings 12-22 59

20th Sunday – Read 2 Kings 63

21st Sunday – Read 1 and 2 Chronicles 67

22nd Sunday – Read Ezra 71

23rd Sunday – Read Nehemiah 75

24th Sunday – Read Esther 78

25th Sunday – Read Job 82

26th Sunday – Read Psalms 86

27th Sunday – Read Proverbs 90

28th Sunday – Read Ecclesiastes 94

29th Sunday – Read Song of Songs 98

30th Sunday – Read Isaiah 101

31st Sunday – Read Jeremiah 105

32nd Sunday – Read Lamentations 110

33rd Sunday – Read Ezekiel 114

34th Sunday – Read Daniel 119

35th Sunday – Read Hosea 123

36th Sunday – Read Joel, Amos, Obadiah 126

37th Sunday – Read Jonah, Micah, Nahum 131

38th Sunday – Read Habakkuk, Zephaniah 136

39th Sunday – Read Haggai, Zechariah, Malachi 139

40th Sunday – Read Matthew 143

41st Sunday – Read Mark 153

42nd Sunday – Read Luke 159

43rd Sunday – Read John 165

44th Sunday – Read Acts 172

45th Sunday – Read Romans 181

46th Sunday – Read 1 and 2 Corinthians 189

47th Sunday – Read Galatians, Ephesians, Philippians 198

48th Sunday – Read Colossians, 1 and 2 Thessalonians 207

49th Sunday – Read 1 and 2 Timothy, Titus, Philemon 214

50th Sunday – Read Hebrews and James 223

51st Sunday – Read 1 and 2 Peter, 1,2,3 John, Jude 232

52nd Sunday – Read Revelation 241

For my girls, Shelley, Rebecca and Rachel

'Righteousness is not just a value; it is God's part of human life, God's stake in human history.'

Abraham Joshua Heschel, 'The Prophets'

Preface

I did not start out to write something others might read. Initially, the work began because my church started a year through the Bible read. Since I had read the bible before, I thought this time I would be more deliberate. So each week for a year, I searched my library for works associated with the assigned Biblical text and read those too. Then I decided to take the effort a step further. I posted a summary of what I had learned on social media for my friends to read. I also posted a photograph with each summary. (What better way to introduce God's word than by posting a visual of his creative side!)

My worldview is Biblical but it has not always been so. It has taken time and immersion in the study of the word of God for this to become true. I would encourage each reader to study the Bible along with this book and to read it slowly over a year. There are a total of 52 posts that cover all the books in the Bible. Some posts are one page and the longest is about eight pages. We are called to be still on the Sabbath and a substantive reading can help do this. My hope is that each of us in our study would truly learn to:

'Love the Lord our God with all our heart, and with all our soul, and with all our might.' Deuteronomy 6:5

In our seeking there will be times of revelation, times of peace and times of frustration. John Wesley, founder of the United Methodist Church once wrote,

'Here then I am, far from the busy ways of men. I sit down alone; only God is here. In His presence I open, I read His Book; for this end, to find the way to heaven. Is there a doubt concerning the meaning of what I read? Does anything appear dark or intricate? I lift up my heart to the Father of lights: 'Lord, is it not thy Word, "If any man lack wisdom, let him ask of God?" Thou "givest liberally and upbraidest not." Thou hast said, "If any be willing to do thy will, he shall know." I am willing to do, let me know thy will. I then search after and consider parallel passages of Scripture, 'comparing spiritual things with spiritual.' I meditate thereon, with all the attention and earnestness of which my mind is capable. If any doubt still remains, I consult those who are experienced in the things of God, and then the writings whereby, being dead, they yet speak. And what I thus learn, that I teach [John Wesley, Preface to Standard Sermons].'

May we all strive to be like Job when he prayed, 'As for me, I would seek God, and to God I would commit my cause.' Job 5:8-9

1st Sunday – Read Genesis 1-5

'Who told you that you were naked? Have you eaten from the tree of which I commanded you not to eat?' Gen 3:11

April 11, 2010

Our Church started a year through the Bible read after Easter. It is really interesting to think about all the large questions of life posed in Genesis. In just a few chapters of Genesis, we are presented with big ideas, not necessarily physics lessons. How did we get here? We believe that God did it, we just don't know how and when. What are we to do while we are here?

'Leave your mother and father, be fruitful and multiply, and till the earth and keep it.' Gen 1:22, 2:15, 3:24 What about others? Cain killed Abel because he was jealous. The Lord told Cain after his treachery. 'Why are you angry, and why has your countenance fallen? If you do well, will you not be accepted? And if you do not do well, sin is couching at the door; its desire is for you, but you must master it?' Gen 4:6-7

Reading the Bible with people in church is cool if for no other reason than it's a place as Merton might say where we can get together and talk about more 'than what's in the icebox, the weather or who's getting a divorce.' Burton Visotzky held a class on the book of Genesis that lasted for 5 years. Radio host Dennis Prager taught a group the first 5 books of the Bible and went through every verse. He reported a few weeks ago that they finished after 18 years.

There is much to learn from the Bible. Some critics selectively pick a verse or two out to point out how weird the Bible is. For those of us who try to read the Bible sincerely and are perplexed, Visotzky in 'Reading the Book' gives us consolation when he writes 'the process of agonizing over the words is what forces them to yield meaning.' The Church has small groups of men and women who have done well by doing this as a main thing in their lives.

2ND SUNDAY – READ GENESIS 6-36

'But Sarah denied saying, 'I did not laugh,' for she was afraid. He said, 'Oh yes, you did laugh.' Gen 18:15

April 18, 2010

I like to think of the Bible as having been written by the wisest of the oldest who ever lived. After the fall of man, we are told two stories that illustrate life without God (Genesis 6-11). Our writers tell us about at a time when 'the Lord saw that the wickedness of man was great in the earth, and that every imagination of the thoughts of his heart was only evil continually. And the Lord was sorry that he had made man on the earth, and it grieved

Him.' Gen 6:5-6 But Noah found favor with the Lord because Noah walked with God. In the tower of Babel, we have story about trying to be God.

The world in which our Bible writers lived was polytheistic. People without radar, doctors and antibiotics believed that if a storm came, the god of weather was ticked off. If you got sick, another god must have been mad. People worshipped anything they could to cover all their bases.

Out of this worldview, God summoned a people to be His own. Abraham was called by God to leave his home and follow God's plan to establish monotheism for the first time. One God did it all. The world and life were not random events that just happened. The Lord did it. In Genesis chapters 12-35, we are taught about the establishment of a people who separate themselves from the worshipping of many Gods. There is but One.

Our Bible writers do not deceive us. We are flawed, Abraham and Sarah laughed at God when they were told they would have a son at an old age. They tried to take matters into their own hands and force the situation through their maid Hagar. Jacob tricked his brother Esau. Laban tricked Jacob and the saga goes on and on.

But the overriding theme is that God wants to have a relationship with us. He came to Abraham to make a covenant. He wrestled with Jacob to make him decide if he would follow or not. God hears our prayers . . . 'I will go down and see if they have done evil according the outcry which has come to me.' Genesis 18:21 Our Bible writers still had to live in the world, but they believed that God was in control and keeping their eye on Him was the best way to go.

3rd Sunday – Read Genesis 37-50

'Even though you intended to do harm to me, God intended it for good.' Gen 50:20

April 25, 2010

In the previous chapters, Genesis 12-36, we learned about the Patriarchs of our faith, Abraham, Isaac and Jacob. Claus Westermann in his book 'Genesis, An Introduction' says in the Patriarchal narratives we are told 'man was created for community.' We learn that 'conflict is part of brotherly existence.' And there is going to be 'tension between children and parents.' Westermann adds that these narratives are vital links because 'what happened to Abraham and Sarah, Isaac, Jacob and Esau, Joseph and his brothers continues to happen with countless variations from one generation to the next.' Westermann sums it all up: 'God made us and He also made the family event and the family relationship and He preserves both.' (Think about what happens when families nurture and love one another; and then what happens when they don't. Or put another way, why you can have all the talent, fame and money in the world, but you're only supposed to have one girl.)

In the remaining chapters of Genesis 37-50, we read about Jacobs sons. The prominent son in this narrative is Joseph. The story is filled with the same conflict and tension we read about from previous generations. Joseph is perceived as arrogant "Behold, I have dreamed another dream and the sun and moon and stars were bowing down to me.' Gen 37:9 His father and brothers rebuked him. The brothers plotted to kill Joseph and eventually sold him as a slave. What is new for me in this narrative according to Westermann is, 'the family story is weaved into a political narrative for the first time. Joseph is sent to Egypt. After more turmoil including being tempted by the Potiphar's wife, he ends up running the Egyptian Department of Agriculture if you will. Good times roll and food is saved. Bad times follow and Joseph's brothers come to Egypt looking for food.

Joseph saw his brothers and really wanted revenge. He set up various plots but in the end wept bitterly, then forgave and reconciled with his brothers. In the meantime, the Department of Agriculture ended up buying everybody's cows and land because people needed food during the drought. We now have a political system that has all its citizens enslaved. As the narrative closes, Jacob blesses his sons who will become the 12 tribes of Israel (several tribes aren't going to be very good though as Jacob describes Ruben as unstable as water and Issachar who saw that resting was good and would become a slave at forced labor). The brothers never can quite get over what they have done to Joseph until he tells them; 'Fear not, for am I in the place of God? As for you, you meant evil against me; but God meant it for good, to bring about that many people should be kept alive.' Gen 50:19-20

4th Sunday – Read Exodus 1-11

'Let my people go.' Exod 5:1

May 2, 2010

This week we read Exodus 1-11. According to Walter Brueggemann in his book 'Old Testament Theology, Testimony, Dispute, Advocacy', we are reminded that the primary subject of the Old Testament is God. We read, think and talk about the Bible to learn about God. And what is written 'is taken by the faithful as revelation, as a true and reliable disclosure of who God is.' From our text this week, we learn of a new King who did not know Joseph and who decided to deal 'shrewdly' with the Hebrew people. Exod 1:10 The new Pharaoh set taskmasters and heavy burdens upon the people. Moses is born under infanticide orders from Pharaoh. It is important to note that women play key roles in Moses surviving the death order. Shiphirah, Puah and the Pharaoh's daughter all decide to buck the system. Still Israel groaned under their bondage, cried out for help and their cry came up to God.

Moses grew up in Pharaoh's house but remembered his heritage. He killed an Egyptian taskmaster. Moses was turned on by two Hebrews and fled to the wilderness. Minding his own business, Moses had an encounter with God at the burning bush. Moses took off his shoes, hid his face and was afraid to look at God. (We might learn something here about our need for experiential worship.) The Lord tells Moses he had heard the people's cry and would send him to get the Pharaoh to set the people free. Moses used the 'but' word many times. But, who am I that anyone would listen, but I am slow of speech (he stuttered), but surely you can send someone else. God agreed to send Aaron along with Moses to deliver the message to the Pharaoh. The Pharaoh heard Moses and Aaron out but he did not let the people go. Instead he increased the burden and said now they would 'make bricks without straw.' Exod 5:7 God sent plagues . . . the Nile turned to blood, frogs, gnats, flies, diseased cattle, boils, hail, locusts, darkness and finally, the death of each Egyptian firstborn child. The Lord asked 'How long will you refuse to let my people go?' Exod 10:3

Gerald Janzen in his commentary on Exodus writes that in the beginning of our text today God is not mentioned. But for those who have learned to recognize the signs, they see God working through the women in the early part of the story. In a sequence in chapter two, we have Israel crying out to God four times. Each time it is revealed that 'God heard, God remembered, God saw, God knew.' Janzen writes that even when we think no one cares 'every cry is falling on the heart of God'. As disclosed to the ancestors, the Hebrews in Egypt are learning about the true character and identity of God, 'a God who is loyal and compassionate; who gives life and nurture and provides a space to live.' God not only hears, but He comes down and enters Moses' everyday consciousness. 'God draws us, has us look at the world differently and then he sends us.'

There are plenty of hard sayings in the Bible. One of the hardest is the fact that God hardened Pharaohs' heart so that he would not let the people go.

Janzen gave me a new way to look at this when he wrote that maybe 'God simply handed Pharaoh over to his own mind-set and the acts it moved him to.' Still the God of the Hebrew Scriptures is not to be trifled with. He 'made spectacle of Pharaoh and his supposed power. Yahweh stands for divine power sufficient to overcome the greatest political power in the world.' Still that way, amen?

5th Sunday – Read Exodus 12-31

'Now I know that the Lord is greater than all gods . . . '
Exod 18:11

May 9, 2010

Exodus 12-31 is some of the most riveting and theologically important text in the Bible. With the final plague about to result in freedom, God instructs the Hebrews to mark their doors with lamb's blood so the 'destroyer' will not enter their homes. As the escape begins, an angel of God follows the Hebrews day and night as they navigate toward the sea. Fear nearly overwhelms the Israelites as Egyptian forces give chase. Moses instructs the people to 'be still' and believe that the Lord will deliver them. With the enemy stuck in the mud, the waters sweep over the Egyptians allowing the slaves to become free (in the desert.) Aaron's sister Miriam leads Israel in its first free celebration in over 400 years.

Only a few days of freedom pass without adequate food and water and the people start to grumble 'Was it because there were not enough graves in Egypt that you brought us out into the desert to die? Exod 14:11 The Bible says the Lord tested them. God began to provide manna (literally means 'what is it') to eat. He instructs them only to gather what they could eat in a day and not to store up for themselves. With the destination the 'mountain of God' Israelite community life begins to march. Moses is spiritual guide and judge. His father in law Jethro (a non-believer) visits and hears all the drama surrounding their new found freedom. Jethro says 'Now I know the Lord is greater than all other gods.' Exod 18:11 Jethro initiates the second celebration reported by bringing a burnt offering to God.

With smoke, fire and thunder the Lord delivers the Ten Commandments and the law to Moses. The laws are wide-ranging, sort of what to do in: personal injury situations, kidnapping, property disputes and about social justice (do not follow the crowd if what they are doing is wrong), and of course observe the Sabbath as a holy day. When the law is received it is time to build a sanctuary so the 'Lord can dwell among you' and to do so with an offering 'from anyone whose heart prompts them to give.' Exod 25:2-8 The text closes with detailed instructions for building the Tent Tabernacle and the Ark of the Covenant which will hold the tablets of instructions inscribed 'by the finger of God.' Exod 31:18

A new connection made for me with the help of Janzen's commentary is the first use of the word congregation. God created the family relationship and now he creates the congregation. Through the ritual of worship, God will sustain both the family and the congregation. Is there any other explanation why this small group of people and the Bible still exist after three thousand five hundred years? Even the great library of Alexandria, charged with gathering all the wisdom in the world, is gone. The Jewish people are still here and the Bible is the number one selling book in the world. Another interesting note is that a woman, Miriam and the outsider Jethro conduct the first two post exodus celebrations. (This in contrast to what the chosen priestly line beginning with Aaron will do in the closing chapters of Exodus). And finally, 'God's laws are another means by which God's gracious providence seems to sustain us in life for our lasting good.'

6th Sunday – Read Exodus 32-40, Leviticus 1-9

'I have seen this people, how stiff-necked they are.' Exod 32:9

May 16, 2010

Exodus 32 -40, Leviticus 1-9

Now while Moses was up on Mount Sinai getting the law from God, the people saw that Moses was taking to long in coming down. They said 'As for this fellow Moses who brought us up out of Egypt, we do not know what has happened to him.' Exod 32:1 So the crowd gathered up all the gold they could find and asked Aaron to make them a statue of a golden calf to worship.

God looks down and says to Moses 'your stiff-necked people' have become corrupt making an idol and bowing down to it. When confronted, Aaron who was in charge while Moses was away says, 'these people are bent on evil . . . they gave me some gold and I threw it in the fire and out came this calf! Moses intercedes for the people. He asks the Lord to remember the covenant and tells the Lord that he will make atonement for the 'great sin' (Exod 32:30) they have committed. Remarkably, after requesting and then being able to see the glory of God, Moses proclaims 'The Lord, the Lord, compassionate and gracious God, slow to anger, abounding in love, and faithfulness, maintaining love to thousands and forgiving wickedness, rebellion and sin.' Exod 34:6 The people are granted a new beginning again. Exodus closes with the final preparations and building of the tent tabernacle.

The first nine chapters of Leviticus set the stage for ritual religious life. The people are told to bring an offering of their first fruits to the Lord. Specifications are laid out for atonement through the sacrificial system for when the people sin either intentionally or unintentionally. When a person screws up, he should first confess that he is guilty and then bring a sin offering to the tabernacle. They are told that if they are wealthy bring their best ram. If one was not as fortunate, then one could bring a goat; less so a dove or pigeon; less so a cup of flour.

The most significant text in this passage is what Janzen calls the second fall of man (golden calf idol) and its implications for us. Through the patriarchs and Moses we discover that we have a loving and gracious God who created this beautiful and bountiful world for us to live. God knew it was not good for us to be alone and so he gave us mates that we might live wholesome lives together. He wants us to be free but in the garden and now at the base of Sinai, we rediscover that there is something dark and sinister involved as well. From whence does this darkness come? God did not attach puppet strings to us. Still, we might not be as free as we think. A dark force exists in this world. It pulls and attracts. We try and fight it off but it seems that without the proper tools we often succumb to its tortuous ways. Janzen puts it this way, 'There is an effective energy and a powerful tendency, not simply originating with us, that works to seduce us into a mind-set and pattern of behavior that amounts to falling short of what we were created and are called to become.'

God gave us the Bible to help us recognize this condition. What to do then? 'Delight in the law of the Lord, and on his law mediate day and night' (Psalm 1:2). My reading helps me feel small for the times I have been disobedient (especially in my youth) and ungracious for the many blessings received. What great luck that we have such a merciful and compassionate Creator that offers new beginnings!

7th Sunday – Read Leviticus 10-27

'If anyone sins- in any of all the things that men do - he shall . . . ' Lev 4:2

May 23, 2010

Leviticus 10-27

Life without Bible reading is like the butterfly above with its wings closed, dull and drab. But life with Bible study is like the butterfly with its wings open, revealing and surprising. Still reading Leviticus in the 21st century seems strange. The rituals and blood sacrifices are images that are foreign to us. Yet, we need to study the Hebrew Scriptures to develop what Richard

Lisher calls a 'linguistic base camp.' We read to develop and understand a biblical worldview. Plus if we didn't read Leviticus we wouldn't know where the term 'scapegoat' comes from (Lev 16:26) or where the second half Jesus' greatest commandment is derived (Lev 19:18). Jesus knew his Hebrew Scriptures and we need to know them too.

Mary Fairchild summarizes Leviticus as teaching us about the Holiness of God, ways to deal with sin, and how to worship. She counted and the word Holiness and it is used 152 times in the book. 'Be holy because I, the Lord your God, am Holy. (Lev 19:2)'. The biblical worldview is that the Israelites and now we are set apart for holiness. Think about the secular approach to life and compare that with the Holy. One the one hand we have 'to take' on the other we have 'to give.' One the one hand we have 'me'; on the other we have 'the other.'

But we still have to deal with the problem of sin. Fairchild writes that 'the sacrifices and offerings detailed in Leviticus were a means of atonement or symbols of repentance from sin and obedience to God.' Not sinning meant more than being good. Leviticus speaks to intentional and unintentional sin. 'When you reap the harvest of your land, do not reap to the very edges of your field or gather your gleanings . . . leave them for the poor and the alien.' (19:9)

In his e-year through the Bible series, Dr. James Howell writes 'Old Testament scholar Walter Brueggemann reminds us that, in the face of guilt, two things must be done. The first is reparation; you must pay back sheep for the sheep you stole or damaged. You cannot merely apologize, or count on insurance to make the problem go away. You leave a hole on your property and a ram falls in and dies, you have to give the owner your best ram. Reconciliation is serious, tangible . . . . there is a second thing to be done which oddly we cannot actually do; it must be done for us. When our relationships are broken, no matter how hard we try; we can never fully repair the damage. Some residue of guilt lingers . . . . Biblical people understood, and believed that only God's power, God's healing energy, released by the sacrifice of something precious, could bridge that gap and finish the healing.'

Reading on in Leviticus we get to the part about blessings and curses (chapters 26-27). 'If you follow my decrees and are careful to obey my commands, I will send you rain in season . . . you will eat all the food you want and live safely in your land.' Lev 26:3-4 On the other hand, 'if you do not listen to me and carry out these commands and if you reject my decrees and abhor my laws and fail to carry out all my commands and so violate my covenant then I will do this to you: I will bring upon you sudden terror, wasting diseases and fever that will destroy your sight and drain away your life . . . . I will make your hearts so fearful that the sound of a windblown leaf will put you to flight.' Lev 26:14-36 God might have concluded here which went unpublished at the time; 'I'm just saying.'

Many Christians don't think much about Old Testament law. Dr. Howell writes 'The thicket of laws that boggle the mind in Exodus and Leviticus pose challenges in interpretation. The Israelites were a nomadic and then an agrarian people – so how do we paved-over urbanites make sense of God's will for goats, turtledoves, and crops? There is great wisdom in striving to delve into the heart of laws that made sense in one cultural setting, and not merely ignore them because we are 21st century technological people, and not Bronze Age herders . . . . We pay heed to all of the law and ask in each instance, what does this commandment reveal about the heart of God? And what does this law tell us about the dark side of human nature – and our noble dreams?'

8th Sunday – Read Numbers 1-10

'Take a census of the congregation of Israelites . . .'
Num 1:2

May 30, 2010

Since Rebecca graduated last week, I took a week off of my reading through the Bible in a year journey. I'm back at it this week with the first 10 chapters of the book of Numbers. The book of 'Numbers' is named so because it begins and ends with a census being conducted. The text for the census is long and arduous to read but meaningful in its inclusion in the Bible. Simply put our ancestors are letting us know that while the Hebrew people are camped in the desert, God's promise to preserve and protect them is still there and the people will not vanish in the wilderness. While the book starts out with a census,' In the Wilderness' is the proper Hebrew title for the book. That title will be evident in the coming chapters but certainly for the first part it's all about numbers. So what was the tally . . . others have added it up and it came to 603,550 males (some surmise a total population of 2 million). We could spend time debating the large numbers but we'll save that for another day. The counting takes about five chapters. (Memo to self: next time remember to make a strong cappuccino before sitting down to read the census in Numbers).

The other five chapters are setting the groundwork so that the Hebrew people learn through worship to have God at the center of their lives before they head off into the wilderness. Among other things, the details of the camp are set out. The tent tabernacle will be in the center of the camp. The Levites who are caretakers of the tabernacle will surround the worship center. Then three tribes will camp in each of the four directions around the camp making up the twelve tribes. Interestingly, according to the Oxford commentary, the Levites are entrusted with 'protecting the tabernacle from casual contact, maintaining the tent, carrying it and pitching it.' With the golden calf episode not to far passed 'safeguards had to be installed.'

There are a couple of more things in the text this week that have significance for me. First is the famous benediction from Num 6:23-26, 'Thus you shall bless the Israelites: You shall say to them, The LORD bless you and keep you; the LORD make his face to shine upon you, and be gracious to you; the LORD lift up his countenance upon you, and give you peace.'

And another prayer from Numbers 10:35, 'Whenever the ark set out, Moses would say, 'Arise, O LORD, let your enemies be scattered, and your foes flee before you.'

And whenever it came to rest, he would say, 'Return, O LORD of the ten thousand thousands of Israel.' Num 10:36 We might learn from these little nuggets that praying was a big deal back then. And that the people believed if they kept an eye of God, He would keep and eye on them.

Lastly I was interested to read about the Nazirite in chapter six which means one 'set apart'. The Levites we remember have been called to be the priestly group and manage temple affairs. But now we have another select group of people who have made a vow to separate themselves to the Lord. A Nazarite would have been known for being a teetotaler and having a really long beard. We have a people that are learning that all their blessings come from the Divine. They pray, give back to God with their physical fruits and labor and now we hear that some dedicate their children solely to the service of God so that they might be trained and ready for a really big assignment down the road.

9TH SUNDAY – READ NUMBERS 11-36

'Then the Lord opened the mouth of the donkey . . . '
Num 22:28

June 6, 2010

A main theme in Numbers is that the people of Israel still don't really believe God would fulfill His promises to them. A pattern throughout Numbers repeats: The people complain that something isn't just right. The Lord's anger burns against the ungrateful lot. The people cry when they are punished. Moses intercedes to the Lord on their behalf. The Lord relents or gives the people a way back (though not without consequences).

For example, the people whine, 'O that we had meat to eat. We remember the fish we ate in Egypt for nothing, the cucumbers, the melons, the leeks, the onions, and the garlic, but now our strength is dried up, and there is nothing at all but this manna to look at.' Num 11:4-6

The Lord replies 'How long shall this wicked congregation murmur against me? 'You want meat; I'll give you meat . . . so much that it will come out your nostrils.' Num 11:18-20

Moses is worn out from carrying the burden of solving all the people's problems. He gives us a good example in that we can have vigorous interaction with God. Moses shows a full range of emotions in his appeals, prayers and requests to God. God listens to Moses and agrees to share the spirit given to Moses with trusted others in the clan.

Another thing that happens a few times in the book is that Moses' leadership is challenged. First it is his own kin Miriam and Aaron who ask Moses why he thinks he is so special. The narrator gives us a clue about the kind of man Moses was and perhaps what it was about him that got God's favor. The narrator reports "Now the man Moses was very meek, more than all men that were on the face of the earth.' Num 12:3 Miriam seemingly contracts leprously for her sin. Moses instead of being smug prays for her "Heal her, O God, I beseech thee." Num 12:13 (And she was).

Israel in its trek across the wilderness gets close to the promised land of Canaan. The Lord directs Moses to send men in to spy on the new land. Only two men (Caleb and Joshua) have the courage to trust that God would safely deliver them to the new land. The people listen to the naysayers and cry out against God again. The pattern mentioned above is repeated. Moses appeals that the people be forgiven. God gives them a way forward but states that only Caleb and Joshua of the living adults would see the Promised Land. The rest of the people including Moses would have to wander for 40 years and would die in the wilderness. (Seems like the people got what they were whining about).

The people also are reminded again to follow the Lord's commandments. They are instructed to write the commandments on tassels and hang them on their clothing. "Follow the commandments of the Lord, not to follow after your own heart, which you are inclined to do wantonly.'

There also are a number of bizarre episodes in the closing chapters of Numbers. Korah rose up to challenge Moses and was swallowed up by the earth. Various battles take place which Israel wins. Israel understood that they were supposed to wipe out all the people and cites of their enemies and keep only the virgin girls. A non-Israelite, Balaam who made a living putting curses of people, is used by God to keep history going in the right direction when the Israelites were bickering among themselves. Balaam is put on the right course by a talking donkey.

Another point to make is that women are often perceived as totally powerless in early Bible times. Well there are two different episodes about the daughters of Zelophehad. The girl's father had died and he had no sons. They challenged the leadership of the day and said it was not fair that they could not inherit their fathers land. Moses consults with God and He concurs that the girls do indeed get to keep the land.

Miriam and Aaron both die and are taken to be with their ancestors. Moses is allowed to go up to Mount Abarim and get a view of the Promised Land. But he will not be allowed to enter. The Lord instructs Moses to select a new leader. When Moses dies, Joshua will be the leader of Israel.

10th Sunday – Read Deuteronomy

'Man does not live by bread alone but from every word from the mouth of God.' Deut 8:3

June 13, 2010

The book of Deuteronomy is known as the 'second law' or re-telling of the story of Israel's foundation. It tells again of the covenant God made with the forefathers. It restates many of the laws given to the people through Moses. And it tells them they will be blessed if they follow the law and cursed if they do not. In the book, Moses reminds the people over and over that it was God who was responsible for the great wonders shown during the exodus from Egypt. It was God who gave them the law and it was God who in a pillar of cloud and fire guided them during the wilderness years.

There are a number of things that are fresh in the book even though most of the same information is covered in the previous four books. Some commentaries suggest that the book was written much later than the first four books and shows growth in theological understanding.

There are a few things that stand out in the re-telling of Israel's story. First is Moses' bold proclamation in chapter 4, 'Now O Israel give heed to the statues and ordinances which I teach you . . . do them . . . keep them and do them.' Isn't it interesting that God's commandments are not something we just know about. They are something which we perform.

In Deut 6:4-9 we have the Shema and they are the most important verses in Judaism:

'Hear, O Israel: The LORD is our God, the LORD alone. You shall love the LORD your God with all your heart, and with all your soul, and with all your might. Keep these words that I am commanding you today in your heart. Recite them to your children and talk about them when you are at home and when you are away, when you lie down and when you rise. Bind them as a sign on your hand, fix them as an emblem on your forehead, and write them on the doorposts of your house and on your gates.'

When Jesus was asked what the greatest commandment was, he searched his knowledge of Hebrew scripture and cited the Shema, Deut 6:4-9 and Leviticus 19:18. (Love the Lord will all your heart and love your neighbor as yourself.)

In chapter 7 we read in the text the proclamation for why God did what He did:

'It was because the LORD loved you and kept the oath that he swore to your ancestors, that the LORD has brought you out with a mighty hand, and redeemed you from the house of slavery, from the hand of Pharaoh King of Egypt.' Deut 7:8

The Lord did what He did because he loves us:

'Know, then, that the LORD your God is not giving you this good land to occupy because of your righteousness; for you are a stubborn people Deut 9:6 He humbled you by letting you hunger, then by feeding you with manna, with which neither you nor your ancestors were acquainted, in order to make you understand that one does not live by bread alone, but by every word that comes from the mouth of the LORD.' Deut 8:3

The middle chapters 13-30 rehash a lot of the stipulations and ordinances that are to be kept. Towards the end of the book the challenge is set: 'I call heaven and earth to witness against you today that I have set before you life and death, blessings and curses. Choose life so that you and your descendants may live, loving the LORD your God, obeying him, and holding fast to him.' Deut 30:19

Moses is without question the greatest figure in the Hebrew Scriptures. Moses dies at the end of Deuteronomy not having been allowed to enter the Promised Land. The Lord secretly buried Moses and 'no man knows where to this day.' Deut 34:6 In contrast we know that Abraham, Sarah and some of the other Patriarchs are buried in the cave at Machpelah. Where is Moses?

11th Sunday – Read Joshua

'Choose this day whom you will serve.' Josh 24:15

June 20, 2010

Joshua

Moses was gone and now Joshua must take up the leadership role for Israel. Joshua was commissioned by God to conquer enemies and enter the land promised to Abraham. We note that the Lord commands Joshua to arise and go! The journey to victory will not be easy thus Joshua is told four times to be strong and very courageous. Joshua is also commanded to remember the law the Moses brought to Israel and to meditate on the law day and night.

Joshua sends spies in to the new land. The town prostitute Rahab hid the spies when the King of Jericho got wind they are inside the city. Carolyn Pressler summarizes the scene this way: 'The narrative of the conquest of the Canaanites and the life of the chosen people in their land begins with the faithful words and saving deeds of Canaanite whore.'

The Lord reminds Joshua before the battles begin: 'This day I will begin to exalt you in the sight of all Israel, so that they may know that I will be with you as I was with Moses.' Josh 3:7 The people agree to follow Joshua and they miraculously cross over the Jordan in a fashion similar to their crossing of the Red Sea while escaping from Egypt. Also, a commander from the army of the Lord comes on the scene and commands Joshua to take off his shoes as he is standing on Holy ground.

The first battle starts with a march around the city walls of Jericho and ends on the seventh day when all the people shout and the walls tumble down. The people of Israel are commanded by God to utterly destroy all the people in Jericho, except Rahab and her family. They are told that all the gold and silver from the city are to be placed in a treasury for the Lord. Achan and his clan disobey this command and bury some of the booty in their tent. The Lord becomes angry because the people commit a great sin once again. Achan is found out and stoned to death.

The middle chapters of Joshua describe brutal battles like the one for the city of Ai. 'When Israel has finished slaughtering all the inhabitants of Ai in the open wilderness where they pursued them and all of them to the very last had fallen by the edge of the sword, all Israel returned to Ai, and smote it with the very edge of the sword.' Josh 8:24 Battles like this take place in about seven more cities.

These battles take place over a number of years. In chapter 13 Joshua notes that he is getting old. All the land that needs to be conquered will take time. So it is time to start dividing the land. Chapters 14-22 describe the division of land among the tribes of Israel.

In the closing two chapters Joshua is ready to retire and die. He retells the story of Israel. The legacy of Joshua as a commander and leader of the conquest of the Promised Land is tempered with this famous advice for the people. 'Choose this day whom you will serve . . . as for me, and my house, we will serve the Lord.' Josh 24:15

Pressler notes 'the themes Joshua raises-warfare, land, leadership, the unity of the people, and the faithfulness of God-are found throughout the book. The understandings of Scriptures are a product of centuries-long conversation. We would do well to understand Joshua and the following book of Judges as theological and political literature rather than merely historical reports . . . We should listen for the theological message more than for the historical, although history is not irrelevant. What then does the text teach us about God.'

We might then conclude from Joshua that God is with Israel at all times. God uses people like Rahab (outsiders, those considered lowly) to move history in the right direction. Each time Israel conquers a new city all the inhabitants are destroyed and the cities burned. Could this mean that in whatever place we live, we need to get rid of all the stuff that keeps us from meditating on the ways of the Lord day and night?

12th Sunday – Read Judges

'The Lord to Gideon, 'Go, I am sending you.' Judg 6:14

June, 27, 2010

The book of Judges is the funniest book in the Bible to me. I chuckle every time I read it. There is plenty not to smile about in the book, but the authors craft stories that show who we are as humans and how God uses humanity despite our funny nature.

The Oxford commentary provides context for the book by saying that the time of Judges was a period before the great Kings of Israel came on the stage and the religious institutions and governments were not yet formed. During this time, 'leaders are swashbuckling bandits whose influence lasts only during their lifetimes, and Israelite groups unite to fight enemies as members of a loosely organized confederation.'

While the previous book of Joshua lets on that the conquest of the Promised Land was swift and total, the book of Judges paints a different picture. Some of the tribes of Israel conquered territory and held it and others did not. Judges describes the conquest as taking place over a long period of time. There were victories and set backs. Looking back over this period, the narrators give us theological themes. God is always faithful in His promises but it is the people who fail to acknowledge God and live according to His ways that gets them in trouble. The people are always getting caught up in modern culture and worshiping images.

The main themes are played out this way. Israel rejects the teachings of Moses. Israel is oppressed under a tyrannical ruler. Israel cries out to God for help. God raised up a judge to do battle against the oppressor. Israel lived in peace and behaved for awhile. When the Judge died, Israel turned their back on God and' behaved worse than their fathers.' These themes are repeated throughout the book. Things that keep getting repeated in the Bible I think make important points.

As the Bible writers looked back over Israel's history, they believed that God was directly involved. We can see how that actually worked during the Judges period with our introduction to the first Judge, Othniel.

'And the people of Israel did what was evil in the sight of the Lord, forgetting the Lord their God and serving Baal's and the Asheroth. The anger of the Lord was raised and he sold them into the hand of Cu'shan'rishatha'im king of Mesopotamia . . . And the people cried to the Lord for a deliverer . . . Then the spirit of the Lord came upon Othniel (Caleb's younger brother) and he judged Israel; he went out to war, and the Lord gave Cu'shan'rishatha'im into his hand . . . so the land had rest for forty years.' Judg 3:7-11

Throughout the rest of Judges we have the same cycle with different judges being raised. The Oxford commentary puts it this way: 'The tales of Israel's insurgency feature various heroes including Ehud the left-handed man; Deborah, the prophet, Jael the female assassin, Gideon, destroyer of the altar of the deity Baal . . . and Samson the superhero of ancient Israelites tradition.'

As I mentioned earlier, the book of Judges is funny. Ehud kills King Eglon in the toilet. After Ehud escapes, the king's staff thinks the king is in the bathroom doing his business. They wait 'to the point of embarrassment' (Judg 3:25) the Bible says before they go in to check on him. Gideon has an encounter with the Divine when God raises him for a mission. Gideon exclaims, 'Pray, Lord, how can I deliver Israel? Behold my clan is the weakest in Manasseh, and I am the least in my family.' Judg 6:15 Gideon wants to believe but can't quite get himself to accept a divine mission without a sign and then another sign from God.

For Samson's part, as a youth he discovers he has great strength and kills a lion with his bare hands. Samson's weakness is women. He uses a riddle that only he knows the answer to try and trick the family of the Philistine woman he married. His wife tries to get Samson to spill the beans. Finally Samson does and he gets in trouble. His rebuttal is hysterical "If you would not have plowed with my heifer, you would not have found out my riddle.' Judg 14:18 Samson befriends another woman Delilah and the same pattern happens again. The Philistines, who hate Samson because he tied three hundred foxes together by their tails and burned their land, get Delilah to ask Samson for the source of his strength. Samson finally tells Delilah it is his hair. Delilah rats him out and that spells the end for Samson.

Theologically, we learn more about the Divine accord from the period of Judges. God uses women too for the shaping of Israel's history. The Spirit of God comes upon people that God chooses to do His work. Regularly, the unqualified and least likely people are chosen to do the Lord's work. And nations that do not hold God at the center of their national life don't last very long.

13th Sunday – Read Ruth

Hesed - Unwarranted faithfulness and loving kindness.

July 4, 2010

In previous books, we have seen God working in miraculous ways. In the book of Ruth we see a more subtle type of His work. Ruth is one of two books in the Bible named after women. So it is significant for its inclusion in a Bible written by men. While the story is beautiful, make no mistake; life was very hard back then.

The book of Ruth is a story of survival. It begins with background on Naomi. Naomi's family had moved from Bethlehem to Moab years earlier due to a famine in the land. While in Moab, her husband and two sons die leaving Naomi with two Moabite daughter's in-law (Orpah and Ruth). Naomi, whose name means delight, is not sure of her future. At one point Naomi is so full of despair that she asks people to no longer call her Naomi but 'Mara' which means bitter.

After her husband and sons die, Naomi decides to move back to Bethlehem because she hears the famine is over. Orpah and Ruth plan to go with Naomi. After just a short way on the journey, Naomi stops and tells the girls to go back to Moab. She tells them they have more of a chance for survival in their own country. Orpah agrees to go back. But Ruth says 'Do not press me to leave you! Or to turn back from following you! Where you go, I will go . . . your people shall be my people, and your God my God, Where you die I will die . . . May the Lord do thus and so to me, and more as well, if even death parts me from you.' Ruth 1:16-17

Naomi acquiesces and she and Ruth head back to Bethlehem. They get back during the barley harvest and Ruth goes out in the fields to glean. It just so happens that the field Ruth picks to glean belongs to Boaz.

Boaz as it turns out is a relative of Naomi. Boaz hears about how Ruth stood by Naomi and how she is now working to get food on the table. Boaz takes an interest in Ruth and tells his men to keep their hands off her. Boaz also gives Ruth some extra stalks of barley to take home to Naomi.

There are a few important points to make here. First, the original hearers of this story would have known about gleaning from Leviticus 19:9-10 which instructs field owners not to go back over their fields once they have harvested but to leave some stalks and grain for the poor. Second, Ruth is a Moabite. The hearers would have also known that Israel despised Moab and considered it an enemy. Third, we are introduced in this story to the Hebrew concept of 'hesed' which means unwarranted loving kindness or faithfulness. We have seen hesed demonstrated twice; once when Ruth refuses to leave Naomi and then when Boaz showed kindness to Ruth the Moabite.

After gleaning and returning home with extra food, Naomi learns that it was her relative Boaz's field. She instructs Ruth to go back to the field and go lay on the threshing room floor by Boaz once he has retired for the night. Boaz interprets this gesture by Ruth to be her showing kindness to him. He decides to get the town counsel together and have someone formally buy the field Naomi's family had left behind in Bethlehem. Boaz gives notice that there is one man who is a closer relative who can buy the land but that with the land, the man must also care for Naomi and Ruth. The closer relative declines so Boaz buys the land and becomes caretaker for Naomi and Ruth. He marries Ruth and they have a child together.

Throughout the book we read several blessings and prayers. Naomi asks the Lord to bless Ruth for coming with her. Boaz asks the Lord to bless Ruth for sticking by Naomi on the journey back to Bethlehem. The underlying theological message is the providence of God. Pressler writes about this in her commentary, 'The right person appears on the scene at just the right moment. People utter blessings and prayers, and the prayers are answered. Human beings act with great generosity and commitment . . . . the story points to God at work in and through ongoing events and human encounters.'

Finally, God continues to use the poor and powerless to carry out His work. In this case it was Ruth the Moabite who becomes the great grandmother of King David.

14th Sunday – Read 1 Samuel 1-16

'Man looks on outward appearances but the Lord looks on the heart.' 1 Sam 16:7

July 11, 2010

1 Samuel 1-16- Eugene Petersen writes his commentary on 1 Samuel that 'our Hebrew ancestors in faith were magnificent storytellers. They don't pull any punches and write only good stuff. All of life is included in the Bible. 'To be human means to deal with God, and that everything we encounter and experience – birth and death, hunger and thirst, money and weapons, weather and mountains, friendships and betrayal,

marriage and adultery – is included, every nuance and detail of it, in dealing with God.' Peterson says that we humans like stories and that is how we learn. He also notes that the primary subject of these stories is God. 'These stories are not about God, they are stories that reveal a world, and existence, in which God speaks and acts, and chooses, and loves, judges and saves. The people that God revealed himself to and had a covenant with, struggle like us. Earlier books had 'page after page of miracles and wonders. But now it is as if we are being weaned from holy miracles . . . The people understand God as penetrating 'all of life, but hiddenly.' 'God, invisible and silent, is often, even mostly, not apparent, but God is no less present.'

The Bible writers didn't give us all the answers in the text. The stories they tell don't shout 'God' at us. The stories draw us in as participants in the story.

We can see how this happens in the beginning of 1 Samuel. We are told of a Hebrew family living the good life. Elkanah had two wives. One was named Hannah and the other was Peninnah. Peninnah had children but Hannah had no children. And Peninnah used this fact to constantly provoke Hannah. Right away we are drawn into the story.

Hannah chooses not to get caught up in the drama. Instead she chose to go the place of worship and pray. Eli the priest observed Hannah praying and he thought she was drunk. Hannah responds 'No, my lord, I am a woman sorely troubled, I have drunk neither wine nor strong drink, but I have been pouring out my soul before the Lord.' 1 Sam 1:15

Hannah was bold. She skipped all the ritual and sacrifice and even the priest and got down on her knees before God. Peterson points out that one woman nags and the other prays. The one who prays changes the course of history.

Hannah prayed for a son and said that if God gives her one, she would dedicate the child to Him. To Hannah, Samuel was born. Samuel was given to Eli the priest to be raised in the church as a servant of God.

Samuel learns from Eli how to listen to God. For his part, Eli didn't do as well with his own sons. They did not walk in his ways 'but took bribes and perverted justice.' 1 Sam 8:3 So, seeing that Eli was getting old, the people didn't want judges anymore and they said 'We want a king like the other nations.' 1 Sam 8:5

God, having raised Samuel for this purpose, uses him to anoint a king. Saul is anointed the first King of Israel. Saul, although handsome and tall, is not sure he is up for the job. Saul replies to Samuel, 'isn't my tribe the least and my family the humblest?' 1 Sam 9:21 Saul hides when it comes time for the anointing and people have to go and find him.

After the anointing ceremony, the spirit of the Lord comes mightily upon Saul and he becomes another man. The people shout 'long live the King.' 1 Sam 10:24 But Saul doesn't last long in his righteousness. He sins twice pretty quickly. Saul is told to wait seven days after his anointing so that Samuel could perform a proper ritual. Saul decided to start the sacrifice ceremony himself. Samuel finds out and harkens 'The Lord sought a man after his own heart.' Your kingdom will end because you have not listened.' 1 Sam 13:14

Not long after this during a skirmish, Saul is instructed not to keep any of the booty from the first battle. Saul keeps some of the livestock. When confronted with this accusation, Saul says to Samuel, 'I have kept the Lord's commandment.' Samuel wryly says 'then what is all this bleating of sheep and lowing of oxen I hear? Saul says, Arrgh! I have sinned! 1 Sam 15:13-14

Samuel hears God again and begins the process to anoint a successor to Saul. God sends Samuel to Jesse. Jesse is told to show all his sons. One by one all the sons are rejected. 'For the Lord sees not as man sees; man looks on outward appearances, but the Lord looks on the heart.' 1 Sam 16:7 One son is left; he is out shepherding the flock.

The least son David is chosen to be the next king. Samuel anoints David and 'the spirit of the Lord comes mightily upon David from that day forward.' In the very next verse we read 'Now the spirit departed from Saul and an evil spirit tormented him.' 1 Sam 16:13-14

Saul will be King for awhile. In his torment he looks for comfort. He asks for his court to send him someone who can play the lyre. David plays the lyre really well and is chosen to play for Saul. I'll pick up with David and Saul next week.

For now, we are left to consider some good people of the Bible. Hannah teaches us to pray. She shows that in the midst of our ordinary human troubles we are to open our hearts to God. Her prayer didn't concern riches but sacrifice. She would give her gift to the Lord. Samuel is portrayed as a good person too. He is trained to listen to God. God responds to fervent prayer and uses those who listen to Him to change history.

Then we have Saul and David. Saul is a tragic figure and we will learn more about him in the closing chapters. David, well he is the most prolific figure besides Moses in the Hebrew Scriptures.

15th Sunday – Read 1 Samuel 16-31

'The soul of Jonathan was knit to the soul of David.'
1 Sam 18:1

July 18, 2010

1 Samuel 16-31- We left 1 Samuel last week with the peasant boy David (anointed but not yet crowned) being invited into King Saul's court to play music. During this time, David went back and forth; playing music for the King then back to Bethlehem to feed his father's sheep. Soon, David hears about a giant Philistine named Goliath. Goliath according to Eugene Peterson stands 'over nine feet tall and his outsized weaponry set him apart

as larger than life.' No one in the Hebrew camp felt they stood a chance as Goliath taunted them. David for his part was unimpressed. Peterson again, 'God was the reality with which David had to deal; giants didn't figure largely in David's understanding of the way the world worked. David volunteers to fight the giant. Saul said to David 'you are not able . . . you are just a boy.' David replies 'but in the fields, whenever a lion or bear came and took a lamb from the flock, I went after it and struck it down.' 1 Sam 17:33-35

Saul agrees to let David fight. Goliath curses David. David says 'You come to me with a sword . . . but I come to you in the name of the Lord of hosts, the God of the armies of Israel, whom you have defiled . . . for the battle is the Lord's and he will give you into our hand.' 1 Sam 17:45-47 Peterson puts the outcome this way 'David, oblivious to what impresses everyone else, picks up five stones from the brook, preaches a sermon of judgment to Goliath that proclaims God's sovereignty over meanness and might, and kills the giant.'

After the battle, King Saul's son Jonathan and David become friends. 'the soul of Jonathan was knit to the soul of David, and Jonathan loved him as his own soul.' 1 Sam 18:1 What a friend to have and soon David would really need one.

At this point, David begins his military service and helps Israel win more battles. The people start to notice David and chant within earshot of Saul 'Saul has slain his thousands, and David his ten thousands.' 'And Saul was very angry. Saul eyed David from that day on.' 1 Sam 18:7-8

Saul at first tries to set up David to be killed. The King challenged David to kill 100 Philistines and circumcise them. The prize would be a girl. David accepts the challenge and according to Peterson 'comes back with a gunny sack of Philistine foreskins and marries Saul's daughter.'

In chapter 19, Saul is no longer subtle in his attempt to kill David. 'And Saul spoke to Jonathan his son and all his servants that they should kill David.' 1 Sam 19:1 Fortunately, Jonathan was in David's corner and warned him that he needed to leave town. David flees to the wilderness and spends the next dozen years or so on the run. Peterson says this is an exceptional time 'everybody, at least who has anything to do with God, spends time in the wilderness (Moses and Jesus).

Peterson points out that 1 Samuel has 15 wilderness stories about David. His first stop is at Nob where he encounters the priest Ahimelech. The priest broke the rules and gave David bread to eat. He also gave David Goliath's sword which had been taken to the sanctuary for safe keeping (and perhaps remembrance).

As David sets out into the wild, he musters a less than impressive following. 'Everyone who was in distress, and everyone who was in debt, and everyone who was discontented gathered to him. And he became captain over them' (about 400 men). 1 Sam 22:2

It is easy to pick on Saul because of his obsessive behavior toward David. And it is easy to get on the bandwagon for David because mostly he has done the right things. But in the wilderness stories there are flashes of opposite behaviors displayed by Saul and David.

One story is set in the wilderness of Engedi. It tells about a time when Saul was chasing David and he went into a cave to relieve himself. David was hiding in the cave. David snuck up on Saul and cut off a piece of his cloak. David confronts Saul and tries to make peace. Saul replies, 'You have repaid me with good; I repaid you with evil.' 1 Sam 24:17 Saul appears soft for a moment but very quickly he is back to his wicked ways.

Another story tells about David's encounter with Nabal and Abigail. The Bible tells us Nabal is surly and mean. His wife Abigail is clever and beautiful. Nabal insults David and David is just about to clean his clock. Abigail intervenes and convinces David not to listen to the unruly Nabal. David says to Abigail 'You have kept me this day from bloodguilt and from avenging myself with my own hand . . . blessed be your good sense.' 1 Sam 25:33

Near the end of 1 Samuel, David and his bandits go back to David's village of Ziklag. He finds that his town has been ransacked. David goes after the Amalekites and defeats them. He gets back all that was taken from them, including his two wives (interestingly not Michal who he was married to before he left Saul's court but Abigail and Ahinoam). David's military fame is now set.

Saul was not so lucky. His sons, including Jonathan, are killed right before his eyes while they were surrounded by the Philistines on Mount Gilboa.

Saul decides that he would rather take his own life rather than be killed. He falls on his own sword. Peterson says 'Saul's end had been a long time in coming, and now it is complete. Saul dies, the first and failed king.'

We will see what David's reaction is to the news of Saul's death and how he fares when we turn to 2 Samuel next week.

16th Sunday – Read 2 Samuel 1-10

'I will make myself merry before the Lord!'
2 Sam 6:21

July 25, 2010

2 Samuel 1-10 - I'm still using Eugene Peterson's Westminster Bible Companion to aid my reading of the books of Samuel. 2 Samuel is the story of King David. Peterson notes that David is mentioned more than 800 times in the Bible. We are reminded by Peterson that while the writing about David in 2 Samuel is prolific, it is not a story primarily about David. It is about God and the human condition which is 'being created and

called, judged and saved by God . . . . But we require a long growing up to realize who we are and the way we are before God.'

So on with the biblical story. King Saul is dead and David is fresh off another military victory. The news of Saul's death reaches David via an Amalekite man. We remember from the ending of 1 Samuel that Saul killed himself. The Amalekite tells David a fabricated story about Saul's death. Peterson writes "There is the story that we know to be true which David does not know (from 1 Samuel 31); and there is the story David is being told which we know is a lie."

David does not fall for the lie. He says 'We're you not afraid to strike down the Lord's anointed?' 2 Sam 1:14 David has the 'messenger' killed. David also continues to show great emotion in life's big moments. He laments Saul and Jonathon in song . . . . 'How the mighty have fallen' and 'I am distressed for you, my brother Jonathan; greatly beloved were you to me. Your love to me was wonderful passing the love of women.' 2 Sam 1:25-26

Soon after, David moves to Hebron and is anointed king of the southern tribe of Judah. The 11 tribes making up the north were known as Israel. They did not recognize David as king. Abner was the guy leading the north following Saul's death. David tries to get Israel to join Judah but the union will not come quickly. It would take a seven year civil war. Well into the civil war, Abner makes a surviving son of Saul, Ishaal king over the northern tribes. Ishaal sleeps with one of Saul's concubines and this move ticks off Abner. Abner decides he will now help David.

David okays Abner's offer for help but says he wants his old wife Michal back. Michal if we remember had been won by David early in 1 Samuel. But after he fled to the wilderness Saul took her back and gave her to another man named Patiel. Abner agrees to give Michal back to David. The Bible says Patiel 'weeps after her all the way to Bahurim.' 2 Sam 3:16

David is learning to master the political and administrative parts of governing. But he has surrounded himself with wilderness hardened berets like Joab to handle the rough stuff. Joab observes the deal David made and doesn't like it so he kills Abner. David is shocked that Joab did this deed but Joab kept him command.

After seven years, David finally consolidates all 12 tribes. The Bible tells us that David became king of Judah at age 30. At age 37, he reconciled all 12 tribes under his government and moved the headquarters to Jerusalem. He ruled there for 33 years.

The elders of Israel anoint David king for the third time (first by God, then the elders of Judah now the elders of Israel). Peterson points out that at each anointing the events happen without David 'pressing his claim . . . . David knows how to wait.' Providence is the picture being painted here.

As a side note, David had a number of children during his seven year reign over the southern tribe in Hebron (we will hear more about Annon, Absalom and Adoniajah later). During his reign in Jerusalem, David fathers more kids (Solomon will stand out from this lot).

In 2 Samuel, the authors portray David as always praying to God before important steps are taken in his life. At this point, David prays about moving the Ark of the Covenant to Jerusalem. God gives David permission for this move. There are two stories inserted here that make important theological points.

Uzzah was in charge of moving the ark. He uses a cart instead of poles which had been the way to move the Ark heretofore. When the Ark starts to slide out of the cart, Uzzah grabs it with his hands. Uzzah is struck dead. Somehow the ark makes it way in to Jerusalem. David is overjoyed 'David danced before the Lord with all his might' we are told. Meanwhile, he wife Michal watched the proceedings from a window above the courtyard. 'Michal the daughter of Saul looked out of the window, and saw King David leading and dancing before the Lord, and she despised him in her heart.' 2 Sam 6:14-16

David must have gotten hot and taken off his tunic during his dance because when he came in the house, Michal exclaimed 'How the king of Israel honored himself today, uncovering himself today before the eyes of his servants . . . as one of the vulgar fellows shamelessly uncovers himself!' David exclaims back 'I will make myself merry before the Lord.' The Bible says 'And Michal had no child until the day of her death.' 2 Sam 6:20-23

Peterson points out that Uzzah was busy 'making church' happen handling all the details for moving the ark. He made changes to protocol that cost him his life. Michal was observing 'church happen' and critiquing it from the sidelines. The rest of her life was barren. All the while the shirtless David was 'doing church' worshipping God with all of this might.

After this David prays about more conquests. The Philistines are destroyed and we do not hear from them again. He whips Moab and several other arch enemies. In between all the human drama (which is more interesting to read about) is a lot of killing. Peterson points out that the story is not about moral living or David as a moral example. It is what Bruggemann calls 'unlaundered history.' These are the men with whom God works. They turn out to be no better or worse than the people with whom he still works, the very ones we face in the mirror every morning and rub shoulders with every day. Holy history is not utopian history . . . . The biblical story, from beginning to end, is told in terms of the social, cultural, political, and ethical world as it is . . . God embraces us, sin and all, in the act of shaping our salvation . . . . the biblical story and the David story, never let us forget-is primarily a God story, not a human story . . . It is a narrative of what God does to save us, not what we do to please God.'

17th Sunday – Read 2 Samuel 11-24

'It Happened Late One Afternoon.' 2 Sam 11:2

August 1, 2010

2 Samuel 11-24 - We pick up the story of King David and the action will be non-stop till the end of 2 Samuel. In the past, I have to admit to having been overly focused on the antics of David in the second half of 2 Samuel and missing the main points. Over the years I have enjoyed cajoling David apologists (for his troubles when they cite his sin Psalm). But after re-reading both Samuels and with the aid of some good commentary (Eugene Peterson) I have learned to look at the David story differently.

We pick up the story after David had united the northern and southern tribes of Israel. He has defeated his major enemies and it seems as if David is on top of the world. Then we read 'it happened late one afternoon when David arose from his couch and was walking upon the roof of the king's house, that he saw from the roof a woman bathing; and the woman very beautiful.' 2 Sam 11:2 Bathsheba was her name. David summons Bathsheba and makes love to her. Bathsheba conceives a child from the union and sends word back to David that she is pregnant.

Peterson writes "a lustful whim ends in an enormous sex and murder crime.' David sends for Bathsheba's husband Uriah who is away fighting a war. David tries to get Uriah to spend the night with Bathsheba but Uriah refuses because his men are still in harms way. So David sends messages to his Army commander Joab. He wants Uriah on the front line of battle. Joab for once follows orders and Uriah gets killed as planned.

Simply put David became corrupt. We can tell, Peterson writes, because of all the sending's (sending for Uriah, sending commands to Joab etcetera). Then God sends the prophet Nathan. Nathan tells David a story about injustice. David falls for the story and condemns the man for the rotten acts in the story being told. Nathan utters the famous line to David 'You are the man!" 2 Sam 12:1

David shows contrition and admits his sins. Nathan tells him that he is forgiven by God but that there will be consequences. 'Behold, I will raise up evil against you out of your own house.' 2 Sam 12:11

David marries Bathsheba and she gives birth to a sick child. David fasts and prays for the child to be healed but the child dies.

After these grave sins, we might easily become indignant toward David. But we should remember as Peterson writes that 'we are all sinners – our sins may differ but the presence and recurrence of sin does not . . . . The biblical revelation is never about commentary or ideas . . . its about actual persons, actual pain, actual trouble, actual sin, you, me, who you are, and what you have done, who I am and what I have done.'

Peterson also remarks that David is unique in his remorse. "David has that double awareness of God and sin. David prayed, was forgiven and took up his life again as God's king.' Many attribute Psalm 51 as David's sin

Psalm. Peterson says there are actually 7 sin Psalms (6, 32, 38, 51, 102, 30, and 142).

Bathsheba ends up having another son with David named Solomon. We will read about Solomon in 1 Kings.

In between relationship troubles, Israel is warring with the Ammonites. "All the time these soul-revealing episodes are being told us, wars are being fought and governments are being administered.' It is easy to presuppose that people of God are not people of the world but this is not true.

In rapid succession, the family troubles go from bad to worse. David's son Ammon rapes his sister Tamar. He lusted mightily after her, took her and then 'with great loathing' 2 Sam 13:15 sent away after the copulation was complete. Tamar is devastated and moves in with another brother Absalom. The Bible tells us that Absalom 'hated' Ammon. 2 Sam 13:22 The weird part of the story is that when David heard about it he got mad but refused to punish Ammon 'because he loved him.' 2 Sam 13:21

For two years, Absalom stores up hate for his brother and plots. Finally, he arranges a banquet to coincide with the sheep shearing seasons end. Absalom has the king invite Ammon. The plan works and when Absalom is sure his brother has had enough to drink, he has his servants kill him.

When David hears the news of Ammon's death he deeply mourns. Absalom fled to Geshur following the murder. Then David's 'heart yearned for Absalom.' 2 Sam 13:39 Peterson adds that the authors of the story help us to see the 'chasm between what David feels and what he does.'

It is fitting to ask why David is so lax is disciplining his sons. It he too busy with politics and governing to give them the time they need? Or is David so remorseful of his own sin that he is unable to come down hard? Isn't there some of us in here somewhere? We don't want to talk to our kids at the dinner table about our youthful foibles lest they think them okay. When they do something wrong, perhaps we think it's not as bad as if someone else's kid had done the deed.

For several more years, Absalom stews, this time about David. Finally, Absalom wants to come home so he sends for David's right hand man Joab. Joab would not come so Absalom set his fields on fire. Joab comes and through trickery gets David to approve of Absalom coming back to Jerusalem, although David would not allow Absalom in his presence.

At this point, there is a major shift in the story as we learn that "Now there was not one so much to be praised for his beauty as Absalom; from the sole of his foot to the crown of his head there was not blemish on him.' 2 Sam 14:25 Also a big deal is made of Absalom wonderful head of hair.

For two more years, while David is tending to governmental affairs, Absalom sat at the front gate of town hearing all of the people's problems. Absalom gained a reputation for being a man of the people. Absalom kissed the people when he met them and told them it was too bad no one from the king's court could help them. He laments "Oh, that I were judge in the land! Then every man with a suit or cause might come to me, and I would give him justice.' 1 Sam 15:4

Peterson notes that 'the long years of yearning for a father's love have turned Absalom into his father's rival.' In between all the gate sitting and dispute settling Absalom hatches a plan for a coup de tat. When the time is right, he asks for permission to go back to Hebron to worship the Lord. What he really has planned is to announce his kingship. Absalom invites David's counselor Ahithophel to come. When the party is underway, Absalom has the trumpets sound announcing his kingship. Ahithophel is now on board with Absalom as most other people appear to be.

Word gets back to David about the coup and he panics. 'The hearts of Israel have gone after Absalom . . . Get up let us flee or there will be no escape from Absalom.' 2 Sam 15:13-14 The main warrior was back in the wild.

An interesting story is inserted here. Some folks try and get David to take the Ark of the Covenant with him. But David is not interested in being king at any cost. He is willing to let God work things out. So the Ark remained in Jerusalem.

David goes back to praying. He prays for the plans of Ahithophel to be 'turned in to foolishness.' 2 Sam 15:31 David also arranges for one of his guys Hushai to get inside the enemy camp.

Absalom is feeling his oats about now. He convenes a war council of sorts to finalize a battle plan to wipe out David. He seeks counsel from Ahithophel and Hushai. Ahithophel gives the better advice but Absalom listens to Hushai who encourages Absalom to go after David himself. We are told by the Bible writers at this point 'for the Lord had ordained the defeat of good counsel so that the Lord might bring ruin upon Absalom.' 2 Sam 17:14

Ahithophel, who by the way is Bathsheba's grandfather, can't stand that his prestige has taken a hit. He hangs himself in shame. Betrayal begets shame. Shame begets suicide. Peterson notes that betrayal is more common in relationships than we might think.

Anyway, David is back in his element. He is hunkered down in the forest. The narrator reports, 'the troops are hungry, and weary and thirsty in the wilderness.' 2 Sam 17:29 David's team develops a battle plan to stave off Absalom. Joab convinces David that he should remain at the rear. David says 'whatever seems best to you I will do . . . deal gently for my sake with the young man Absalom. And all the people heard when the king gave orders to all the commanders about Absalom.' 2 Sam 18:15

Who is this David? Peterson points out that he is being hunted like an animal for the second time in his life. He was hunted first by Saul, and then by his son Absalom. David is as compassionate with Absalom as he was with Saul.

The battle is joined. Absalom leads the charge. Racing through the forest, Absalom's bountiful hair got caught on oak branches and he was jerked off his mount. Absalom was left hanging in mid air. First on the scene is David's commander Joab. So much for orders; Joab gives Absalom three spears to the heart.

As we would expect by now, David deeply mourns the news of Absalom's death. 'Oh my son Absalom, my son, my son Absalom would that I had died instead of you. O Absalom my son, my son! 2 Sam 18:33

After things settle down, David becomes king again. There are a couple of stories at the end of 2 Samuel that complete the picture being painted. There are stories about of couple of averages Joes (Rizpah and Aranuh). Their plights are brought to the attention of David. David feels compassion and comes to their aid. Peterson points out that people on the margins are essential to God's story. God's story is not about the best happening for the 'brightest' but a reminder of what power should be used to accomplish.

Peterson provides some concluding remarks about David. 'The significant thing about David is his relationship to God. David believes in God, thinks about God, imagines God, addresses God and prays to God . . . . He also forgets, disobeys, sins and ignores God too. But God is the largest part of David's existence.'

I would sum up the story of David by saying that he was a man of passion and compassion; passion for God and compassion for other people. David got off track a few times that's for sure. But David wasn't a holy priest holed up in the sanctuary. David lived his life and had his eye on God. And throughout David's life, we see that God's promises of providence hold up.

18th Sunday – Read 1 Kings 1-11

'As Solomon grew old, his wives turned his heart after other gods.' 1 Kings 11:4

August 8, 2010

1 Kings 1-11 – Sources: The Bible and Terence Fretheim's WBC. King David is old and cold; he can't even die in peace (though he is given a 'warm' blanket). Three of his sons had first names that started with an 'A.' Annon and Absalom made their messes in 2 Samuel. Now the third 'A' son, Adonijah takes his turn. With David confined to a bed, Adonijah proclaims himself king. Quickly upon hearing this news Bathsheba and

the prophet Nathan get to David. They have David remember a promise that he made to Bathsheba, that her son Solomon would be king. David proclaims Solomon king and Adonijah backs down without a fight.

Before he dies, David gives charge to Solomon, 'I am about to go the way of all the earth, he said, So be strong, show yourself a man, and observe what the Lord your God requires. Walk in his ways, and keep his decrees and commands . . . so that you may prosper in all you do and wherever you go, and that the Lord may keep his promise to me: If your descendents watch how they live, and if they walk faithfully before me with all their heart and soul, you will never fail to have a man on the throne of Israel.' 1 Kings 2:2-4

David mentions to Solomon a few scores that need to be settled and then he dies. 'So Solomon sat on the throne of his father David.' 1 Kings 2:12 Solomon's first act as king was to kill his brother Adonijah. His second act was to kill David's old army commander Joab. His third act was to kill Shimel. We are told 'the kingdom of Solomon was now firmly established in Solomon's hand.' 1 Kings 2:12 Solomon's then proceeded to make a peace treaty with the Pharaoh of Egypt and marry his daughter. (A big foreshadow here).

Solomon hears the voice of God in a dream. God tells Solomon to ask for whatever he wants and it will be given him. Solomon replies 'give your servant a discerning heart to govern your people and to distinguish between right and wrong.' 1 Kings 3:9 God is impressed with the request so the Lord says he will give Solomon riches and a long life as well as wisdom.

We have a story inserted here to typify Solomon's wisdom. One woman steals another woman's baby. Both come before the king claiming to be the real mother. Solomon asks for his sword so he can split the baby in half to give each woman a share. The real mother says no; give the baby to the other woman. Solomon wisely chooses the real mother to give the baby.

Solomon's early reign was a peaceful time. Everyone was prospering. All the 12 tribes took turns bringing provisions to supply palace life. Solomon had 4,000 stalls and 12,000 horses. There was a big group of royal people and animals to feed.

The Bible tells us that Solomon had no equal when it came to knowledge, 'God gave Solomon wisdom and very great insight, and a breadth of understanding as measureless as the sand on the seashore.' He was a prolific writer penning 3,000 proverbs and 1,005 songs. Plus 'He described plant life from the cedar of Lebanon to the hyssop that grows out of walls. He also taught about animals and birds, and reptiles and fish. Men of all nations came to listen to Solomon's wisdom.' 1 Kings 4:29-34

With Solomon's credentials established, he would begin making alliances with several neighboring kings to supply materials for the building of a proper temple for the Lord.

'In the year four hundred and eightieth year after the Israelites had come out of Egypt . . . he began to build the temple of the Lord.' 1 Kings 6:1 King Solomon conscripts nearly 200,000 men for the building of the temple and his royal palace. Extensive descriptions are provided for the building of the temple in chapters 5-7. The Bible tells us it took 11 years to build the temple. 'It took Solomon 13 years, however, to complete the construction of his palace.' 1 Kings 7:1

When the temple was complete, the Ark of the Covenant was brought to the new building and placed in the inter sanctum, the Most Holy Place (Holy of Holies). 'There was nothing in the Ark except the two stone tablets that Moses had placed in it at Horeb.' 1 Kings 8:9 With the building complete, Solomon led a temple dedication. Solomon's long prayer recounted the promises God has made to Israel and requests 'O Lord my God, hear the cry and prayer that your servant is praying in your presence this day.' 1 King 8:14-16 The prayer also lifted a number of petitions to God anticipating bad things that could happen and asked for the Lord to help them in bad times. Interestingly to the keen Bible reader is a long paragraph in the prayer asking God to hear the prayers of foreigners as well. In kingly fashion Solomon concludes the eloquent oratory with these words, 'be near the Lord our God day and night, that he may uphold the cause of his servant and the cause of his people Israel according to each day's need, so that all the peoples of the earth may know that the Lord is God and that there is no other.' 1 Kings 8:40

The Lord appears to Solomon again in a dream following the dedication, saying that he will be there for them. The Lord reminds Solomon that if he screws up, the Lord will 'cut off Israel from the land I have given them.' 1 Kings 9:7

Chapter 10 is a transitory chapter, it tells of Queen Sheba visiting Solomon and confirming that all she had heard about his wisdom was true. The Bible writers report that Solomon had amassed a fortune in gold. He made shields of gold and a great throne inlaid with ivory and overlaid with gold for the palace. 'Solomon was greater in riches and wisdom than all the other kings of the earth.' 1 Kings 10:23

King Solomon, however, loved many foreign women besides Pharaoh's daughter-Moabites, Ammonites, Edomites, Sidonians, and Hittites. Solomon had amassed 1,000 wives. 'As Solomon grew old, his wives turned his heart after other gods, and his heart was not fully devoted to the Lord his God, as the heart of David his father had been.' 1 Kings 11:4

The Lord said to Solomon 'Since this is your attitude and you have not kept my covenant and my decrees, which I commanded you, I will most certainly tear the kingdom away from you and give it to one of your subordinates.' 1 Kings 11:11 This is the last communication God will have with a king. All further communication with God will come from a prophet.

19th Sunday – Read 1 Kings 12-22

'How long will you go limping along with two different opinions?' 1 Kings 18:21

August 15, 2010

1 Kings 12-22 – We left 1 Kings after the Lord had proclaimed Israel's 3rd king, Solomon unfit for further duty due to his idolatry. The proclamation stated that the Lord would raise up adversaries against a united Israel.

So this guy Jeroboam was contacted by the prophet Ahijah. The prophet relayed a message from God, 'See, I am going to tear the kingdom out of Solomon's hand and give you ten tribes.' 'I will give one tribe to his son so that David my servant may always have a lamp before me in Jerusalem, the city where I chose to put my Name.' 1 Kings 11:31-36 Solomon's last act was to try and kill Jeroboam. The plot failed but it did force Jeroboam into exile.

The narrator now gets us used to a rapid fire change in leadership that will occur repeatedly throughout the rest of 1 and 2 kings (40 kings over 400 years). He reports 'As for all the other events of Solomon's reign-all he did and the wisdom he displayed- are they not written in the book of the annals of Solomon.' Solomon's reign lasted 40 years and then he died. 1 Kings 11:41-43

After Solomon's death, his son Rehoboam made an effort to keep the 12 tribes together. He sent for Jeroboam in exile. 'The whole assembly of Israel went to Rehoboam and said to him, 'your father put a heavy yoke on us, but now lighten the harsh labor and the heavy yoke, and we will serve you.' 1 Kings 12:4

Rehoboam asked the advice of the elders. They said to him 'If today you will be a servant to these people and serve them and give them a favorable answer, they will always be your servants.' 1 Kings 12:7 Rehoboam did not like this answer so he asked his young friends. They advised him not to lighten the load but to make it harder. 'My father laid on you a heavy yoke; I will make it even heavier. My father scourged you with whips; I will scourge you with scorpions.' 1 Kings 12:11

There was a rebellion and the northern tribes went back home. Rehoboam escaped to Jerusalem. The northern tribes make Jeroboam king. Rehoboam kept the southern tribe of Judah (and Benjamin).

Soon though, Jeroboam got to thinking that all the people would want to go down to Jerusalem to worship at the temple. He figured that Rehoboam would gain favor that way so he made golden calves for the tribes to worship in the northern cities of Bethel and Dan.

There is a bizarre story inserted next to illustrate the role that prophets of God will play going forward. 'By the word of the Lord, a man of God came from Judah to Bethel, as Jeroboam was standing by the altar making an offering. He cried out against the altar by the word of the Lord.' ` Kings 13-1 Fretheim points out that the story illustrates how God will communicate going forward through the prophets. And that it will still be necessary to discern between genuine and false prophets. Further Fretheim adds, we should remember that the words of the Lord through the prophets still left room for people to act faithfully or not.

As we might expect, even after being visited by a prophet, the northern king 'Jeroboam did not change his evil ways . . . . anyone who wanted to become priest he consecrated for the high places. This was the sin of the house of Jeroboam that led to its downfall.' 1 Kings 13:33

The southern king of Judah Rehoboam did not fare any better. 'Judah did evil in the eyes of the Lord. By the sins they committed they stirred up His jealous anger more than their fathers had done.' 1 Kings 14:22

There was continual warfare between the north and the south. When Jeroboam and Rehoboam died, new kings took over. The Bible reports that most did evil in the eyes of the Lord. One king Abaz was so bad 'He even made his son pass through fire, according to the abominable practices of the nations whom the Lord drove out before the people of Israel. 2 Kings 16:3

At this juncture, God sent his first major prophet Elijah on the scene. Elijah proclaimed to the land that because of their unfaithfulness, there would be neither dew nor rain for several years.

Next we have a couple of stories that establish prophetic credentials. Elijah is provided for by the Lord while the famine is underway. He meets a widow who has only a small jar of flour and asks her to fix him something to eat. She says 'I am gathering a few sticks to take home and make a meal for myself and my son, that we may eat it-and die.' 1 Kings 17:12 Elijah says the Lord will provide and the jar of flour will not run dry. It didn't either. Later the woman's son dies, but Elijah prays over the boy and he comes back to life. Elijah is the real deal.

The central text from these passages comes from chapter 18 when Elijah is giving king Abad words from the Lord. Ahab says to Elijah, 'Is that you, O troubler of Israel?' 1 Kings 18:17 Elijah responds, 'I have not made trouble, but you and your father's have. You have abandoned the Lord's commands and followed the Baal . . . . How long will you go limping with two different opinions? If the Lord is God, follow him; but if Baal, follow him.' Elijah sets up a test to demonstrate that God is more powerful than

Baal. The idols do not respond "O Baal, answer us! But there was no voice, and no one answered . . . Cry aloud, for he is a god; either he is musing, or he is on a journey, or perhaps he is asleep and must be awakened.' 1 Kings 18-27 Elijah prays and God responds with fire. God keeps giving people notice. But the leadership didn't like the message and they chased away the prophet.

Next it was Jezebel who had people start chasing Elijah. Elijah got tired of the fleeing and took respite in a cave. Elijah listens for God 'but the Lord was not in the wind . . . and not in the earthquake . . . and not in the fire . . . After the fire came a gentle whisper . . . and Elijah heard it.' 1 Kings 19:11-15 The Lord told Elijah to go back.

At this point, Elijah gets an understudy named Elisha. Elisha left the fields he was plowing to start his master's of prophetic administration under Elijah.

Finally, Elijah girds himself up like a man and goes back to confront King Ahab. 'Ahab said to Elijah, so you have found me, my enemy. I have found you, Elijah answered, because you have sold yourself to do evil in the eyes of the Lord.' 1 Kings 21:20 As it was predicted, King Ahab's suffered a bloody death. New kings kept taking over that did evil in the sight of the Lord.

20th Sunday – Read 2 Kings

Let me inherit a double portion of your spirit.'
2 Kings 2:9

August 22, 2010

2 Kings – We are nearing the end of Elijah's reign as one of the first Major Prophets. Elijah received word from an angel of the Lord to pronounce judgment on king Ahaziah who has just had a bad accident. 'Is it because there is not God in Israel that you are going off the consult Baal? Therefore, this is what the Lord says, 'you will not leave the bed you are laying on. You will certainly die!' 2 King 1:3-4 And the king promptly died.

We learn more about the person of Elijah and his status before his reign ends. 'He was a man with a garment of hair and with a leather belt around his waist.' 2 Kings 1:8 It sounds like he might have been a Nazarite (one dedicated to God). We are told this right before 'the Lord was about to take Elijah up to heaven in a whirlwind.' 2 Kings 2:1 Elijah tries to get Elisha to stay away from him because he will soon be gone up. But Elisha is committed to staying by Elijah's side. Right before the ascension Elijah asks Elisha, 'Tell me, what I can do for you before I am taken from you.' Elisha responds 'let me inherit a double portion of your spirit.' Elijah says back, 'You have asked a hard thing . . . yet if you see me when I am taken from you it will be yours-otherwise not.' 2 Kings 2:9-10

'Suddenly a chariot of fire and horses of fire appeared and separated the two of them, and Elijah went up to heaven in a whirlwind.' Elisha saw this and cried out, my father! My father! The chariots and horsemen of Israel! And Elisha saw him no more.' 2 Kings 2 11-12

We are starting to get the hang of the book of king writers. They tell several stories at this point to establish the credentials of Elisha who will carry on for Elijah. I should not say this, but one of my favorite stories in the whole Bible comes next. 'From there Elisha went up to Bethel. As he was walking along the road, some youths, came out of the town and jeered at him. Go on up, you baldhead they said, Go on up you baldhead! He turned around, looked at them and called down a curse on them in the name of the Lord. Then two bears came out of the woods and mauled 42 of the youths. And he went on to Mount Carmel and from there returned to Samaria.' With a double share of Elijah's spirit, Elisha is not to be trifled with. 2 Kings 2:23-25

WBC author Tim Fretheim points out that Elisha performs more and wilder miracles than does Elijah including feeding 100 hungry men with 20 loaves of bread. The servant asked 'How can I set this before 100 men? Elisha responds 'Give it to the people to eat. For this is what the Lord says, They will eat and have some left over . . . and they ate and had some left over, according to the word of the Lord.' 2 Kings 4:42-44

I'd like to dwell on the miracles. There are number of ways that modern readers interpret them. Some call them symbols. Others read them literally and think they might have happened in Bible times but they don't see them as being credible evidence for the existence of God today.

I will quote Fretheim at length here: "Remarkably, these miracles are not presented in terms of divine intervention, or a violation of the natural order of things, or a disruption of God's creation. Indeed, these matter-of-fact stories witness that God's good creation is properly at work in the midst of those who would disrupt it. They (Bible writers) are remarkably unconcerned to explain how these miracles take place. Modern physics (quantum mechanics, chaos theory) has helped us see that this world is not a closed system of cause and effect, there is a loose, if complex, causal weave or 'play' within God's design that make novelty, freshness, surprise, and serendipity possible. Even more, such a world make it possible for God to be at work within the interplay of natural law and the loose weave. God's creation is not fixed and static, but full of surprises and new possibilities.

He concludes by saying that historians are always trying to sort out 'whether these particular miracles occurred, but they can not with integrity begin by saying they could not happen. One key to understanding is that the Creator has placed within this world human beings with compassion and remarkable gifts who can bring life and well-being to those in need. Each of these stories involves human activity; a prophet enters into the life of another and seeks to ameliorate his or her life situation . . . . They make clear that there are possibilities for life and healing in God's world that go beyond our present calculations and understanding, and they give us hope that God's working in this world through people like ourselves may indeed make miracles happen.'

Chapters 8-24 begin the downward spiral to the end of Israel's existence as a nation. King after king is listed as being more evil than his predecessor. Every now and then a king consults a prophet. Most of the time, the kings do not listen to the words of God.

The northern kingdom of Israel falls to Assyria in 721BC. The people of the north worth keeping were dispersed into other cities. Ten tribes will be gone for good. In chapter 17, the Bible writes go to great length to explain this catastrophe. 'They would not listen but were stubborn, as their ancestors had been who did not believe in the Lord their God. They despised his statues, and his covenant that he made with their ancestors, and the warnings he gave them . . . Therefore, the Lord was very angry with Israel and removed them out of his sight; none was left but the tribe of Judah alone.' 2 Kings 17:13-18

The south continued to hang on for another hundred years or so. During this time, there were a couple of good kings (Hezekiah and Josiah for example) who tried to reform things. But there were still some really bad ones like Manasseh, 'He did what was evil in the eyes of the Lord . . . He erected altars to Baal . . . He passed his son through fire, practiced astrology and read omens, and performed necromancy and conjured spirits. He was profuse in doing what was evil in the eyes of the Lord, to anger Him." 2 Kings 21:3-6 In 587BC King Nebuchadnezzar of Babylon overthrows Judah. Fretheim writes 'Nebuchadnezzar takes all the treasuries of the temple . . . and deports the cream of Judah's society to Babylon.'

I watched the movie 'The Book of Eli' recently. I couldn't help but draw an analogy from the movie as I was concluding this study. The evil character in the movie finally gets a hold of the last Bible on earth. He has sacrificed most of those close to him to get it. When he opens the Bible he coveted, he finds that it is written in Braille. His asks his blind wife who he has severely mistreated to read to him. She says she can't remember how. Then she says 'You have in your hands the book you have always wanted, but it may as well be a million miles away.' For the people of Israel during the time of the kings it was the same.

21st Sunday – Read 1 and 2 Chronicles

'We do not know what to do, but our eyes are upon thee.'
2 Chr 20:12

August 29, 2010

1 and 2 Chronicles - At first glance, 1 and 2 Chronicles appear to cover the same ground as 1 and 2 Kings. They do sort of but with different twists. Where Kings is considered a political history, Chronicles is considered a religious history of Israel. There are several others differences as well.

In Kings, the story and plight of the northern kingdom is told. In Chronicles, the northern kingdom is virtually ignored. With this insight, we get a further sense of the writer's purpose. Chronicles was written after Israel's exile (between 450-400BC). King Cyrus of Persia had defeated the Babylonians and some Jews were returning to Jerusalem. There was talk of rebuilding the temple which had been destroyed by the Babylonians. The chroniclers wanted to set down in writing the proper lineage for kingship and managing temple matters.

So 1 Chronicles is the story of King David told with this view in mind. It begins with a series of genealogies establishing David's pedigree. Adam and Eve had Seth (Cain and Abel are skipped over). Noah's had his boys; Shem, Ham and Japeth. And the list goes all the way to David's great grandfather Boaz. Then Boaz and Ruth had Obed. Obed had Jesse. Jesse was the father of seven sons the seventh of which was David. In all we get nine chapters of genealogies. The lists tell whose line is proper for kingship and lists of all the Levities who have managed temple affairs.

The reign of Saul is covered very briefly. The majority of the rest of the book tells the story of David (his warriors, wars, decision by God not to allow David to build the temple and David's sin of ordering a census). Interestingly, Chronicles omits the story of David and Bathsheba and most of the family drama.

Also interesting to me is the first direct mention of Satan in the Bible. 'Satan stood up against Israel, and incited David to number Israel.' 1 Chr 21:1 The New Oxford Bible says this about the verse, 'Satan replaces 'the anger of the Lord.' During the more than five hundred years since the writing of the earlier account, a considerable theological change had taken place. In the thinking of Biblical men, God came to be considered as only doing good and the figure of Satan was developed to account for evil and misfortune.'

Another difference between Kings and Chronicles is David's involvement with the building of the first temple. In Chronicles we are given new information. We are told that David designed the temple and began to stockpile construction materials that would be used. "He then gives charge to his young son Solomon 'My son, I had it in my heart to build a house to the name of the Lord my God. But the word of the Lord came to me saying "you have shed much blood and have waged great wars; you shall not build a house . . . but your son . . . He shall build a house for my name . . . . Be strong, be of good courage. Fear not; be not dismayed.' 1 Chr 22:11-13

2 Chronicles starts out with Solomon building the temple. Elaborate details are provided. 'The vestibule in front of the nave of the house was twenty cubits long, equal to the width of the house, and its height was a hundred and twenty cubits. He overlaid it on the inside with pure gold.' 'In the most holy place he made two cherubim of wood and overlaid them with gold.' 2 Chr 3:4-8

As was the case with the 1 Chronicles, there is more detail also about the priestly group 'Now when the priests came out of the holy place . . . all the Levitical singers arrayed in fine linen, with cymbals, harps and lyres, stood east of the altar with a hundred and twenty priests who were trumpeters and it was the duty of the trumpeters and singers to make themselves heard in unison in praise and thanksgiving to the Lord . . . . And the song was raised, with trumpets and cymbals and other musical instruments, in praise to the lord 'For he is good, for his steadfast love endures forever.' 2 Chr 5:11-13

Solomon dedicated the temple and we read again that "Solomon excelled all the kings of the earth in riches and wisdom.' We are also told if we want to learn more "Now the rest of the acts of Solomon, from first to last, are they not written in the history of Nathan the prophet, and in the prophecy of Ahijah the Shilonite, and in the visions of Iddo the seer concerning Jeroboam the son of Nebat?' 2 Chr 9:29

As mentioned earlier the history of the northern kingdom is skipped over in Chronicles. The interest of the Chronicler is to provide lineage of the kings who follow in the line of David. Special attention is given to five pretty good kings, Asa, Jehoshaphat, Joash, Hezekiah, and Josiah who all tried to reform a broken monarchy. Ultimately though, history will not be changed. The northern kingdom is defeated and the southern kingdom falls to the Babylonians. And the temple is destroyed.

A final difference between Kings and Chronicles comes at end. After about 70 years in exile we learn that a decree has been issued from Cyrus who appears to be more favorable towards the Jewish people. The Bible says, 'Thus says Cyrus king of Persia, The Lord, the God of heaven, has given me all the kingdoms of the earth and he has charged me to build him a house at Jerusalem, which is in Judah. 'Whoever is among you of all his people, may the Lord his God be with him. Let him go up.' 2 Chr 26:23 Ezra which comes next in the Protestant Bible will pick up here.

22nd Sunday – Read Ezra

'Ezra then was called to teach them the word.'
Ezra 7:10

September 5, 2010

Ezra – At the end of Chronicles we learned that the political guard had changed. Out are the Babylonians who conquered Judah and in is King Cyrus of Persia. King Cyrus seems to be more hospitable toward the Jews. The book of Ezra begins the same way Chronicles ends. "The Lord stirred up the spirit of King Cyrus of Persia so that he sent a herald throughout all his kingdom, and also in a written edict declared:' Ezra 1:1 The Lord has charged me to rebuild the house of the Lord in Jerusalem. We learn that 'survivors, in whatever place they reside . . . got ready to go up and rebuild the house of the Lord in Jerusalem.'

Various commentators point out that the chronology of events in Ezra and the other books of the Hebrew Scriptures don't exactly flow in order. We are going to be reading in the remaining books of the Hebrew Scriptures about times when Israel was in exile and about the faithful people God called to the kings and people of that time. Sometimes the characters even overlap in the stories.

So we should think about a people in exile. An old evil regime got defeated and a new regime that allowed indigenous people to practice their religion came to power. Israel has intermingled over the years and her people had forgotten the words and practices of her forefathers.

So we pick up in Ezra when the people were allowed to begin work on rebuilding the temple after several generations in exile. In chapter three the foundation of the new temple is laid and a great celebration is reported. 'The Levites and heads of families, old people who had seen the first house on its foundations, wept with a loud voice when they saw this house, though many shouted aloud with joy, so that people could not distinguish the sound of the joyful shout from the sound of the people's weeping.'

As my father-in-law is fond of saying 'No good deed goes unpunished.' And so it was during this time when a group of locals emerged who were not fond of the idea that the temple be rebuilt. 'Then the people of the land discouraged the people of Judah, and made them afraid to build, and they bribed officials to frustrate their plan. They did this until the end of the reign of Cyrus.' Ezra 4:4

Then we learn that a new king whose name was Darius came to power. The local Persians wrote a letter to underlings of the Darius administration, 'if this city is rebuilt and the walls finished, they will not pay tribute, custom, or toll and the royal revenue will be reduced. You will discover in the annals that this is a rebellious city, hurtful to kings and provinces, and that sedition was stirred up from long ago.' The underlings of Darius seek to table the rebuilding effort writing back, 'Therefore, issue an order that these people be made to cease, and this city not be rebuilt until I make a decree.' Ezra 4:13-18

Then the Jews got their legal team involved. They wrote directly to King Darius and asked him to search the annals for a decree from King Cyrus. He did this and granted the Jews permission to continue the project. 'Let the work on this house of God alone; let the governor of the Jews and the elders of the Jews rebuild this house of God on its site.' Ezra 6:7

'So the elders of the Jews built the house and prospered, through the prophesying of the prophet Haggai and Zechariah . . . . they finished on the third day of the month of Adar in the sixth year of the reign of King Darius. The people of Israel, the priests, and the Levites, and the rest of the returned exiles, celebrated the dedication of this house of God with joy.' Ezra 6:14-16

In exile the people had forgotten and there must have been some inconsistent lifestyle and worship practices going on. This is when God called for Ezra. 'This Ezra went up from Babylonia. He was a scribe and skilled in the Law of Moses that the Lord the God of Israel had given; and the king granted him all that he asked for, for the hand of the Lord his God was upon him. Ezra then was called to teach them the word. 'For Ezra had his heart to study the law of the Lord, and to do it, and to teach the statues and ordinances in Israel.' 7:6-7

Ezra took stock of the situation in and around the new temple. He issued his own proclamation that the Jewish people should fast and pray. He did this because he found that the people had not been faithful. 'The people of Israel, the priests, and the Levites, have not separated themselves from the peoples of the lands with their abominations, from the Canaanites, the Hittites, the Perizzites, the Jebusites . . . For they have taken some of their daughters as wives for themselves and for their sons. Thus the holy seed has mixed itself with the peoples of the lands, and in this faithlessness the officials and leaders have led the way.' Ezra 9:1-2

Ezra is saddened to see this and prays 'Oh my God, I am too ashamed and embarrassed to lift my face to you, my God, for our iniquities have risen higher that our heads and our guilt has mounted up to the heavens.' The prayer continues 'But now for a brief moment favor has been shown by the Lord our God, who has left us a remnant, and given us a stake in his holy place, in order that he may brighten our eyes and grant us a little sustenance in our slavery.' Ezra 9:5-8

After Ezra prayed and made confession, weeping and throwing himself down before the house of God,' Ezra 10:1 the people agree to send away all the wives and children of the foreigners.

Some people made excuses why they could not do this, 'but the people are many and it is a time of heavy rain; we cannot stand in the open. Not is this a task for one day or for two, for many have transgressed in this manner.' Ezra 10:13 But a faithful few did separate themselves. Ezra closes with a list of the families who did.

23rd Sunday – Read Nehemiah

'Oh, my God, remember to my credit all that I have done!' Neh 5:19

September 12, 2010

Nehemiah – There was a time in Bible academia when scholars thought that Ezra and Nehemiah was originally one book because both cover the same story. But more recent analysis suggests the works are independent.

In the opening we learn that Nehemiah was distressed over the destruction of his homeland. He intercedes in prayer for his fellow countrymen, 'O Lord, God of Heaven, great and awesome God . . . let your ear be attentive and your eyes open to receive the prayer of your servant that I am praying to you . . . . confessing our sins . . . be mindful of the promise you gave to your servant Moses . . . . O Lord, let your ear be attentive to the prayer of your servants who desire to hold your name in awe.' Neh 1:5-11

At the time, Nehemiah was working as a wine taster for the Persian king. He decided to ask for a leave of absence so he could back to help rebuild the wall of Jerusalem and its gates. This request was granted and with permission slip in hand Nehemiah went back to the Province across the river (Jerusalem). Somehow he became governor of the city.

When he got back, he surveyed the damage and convened all the Jews who had returned and said' let us start rebuilding.' Even with a letter from the Persian king granting permission, some locals did not want the building. 'What are the miserable Jews doing? Will they restore, offer sacrifice, and finish one day? Can they revive those stones out of the dust heaps burned as they are? Neh 4:2

Despite the opposition, they began to rebuild the gates. The Sheep Gate, Fish Gate, Old Gate, Valley Gate, Dung Gate, Fountain Gate, House Gate and the Muster Gate are listed as having been restored.

Nehemiah appears to have had an administration which operated based on compassion. 'There was a great outcry by the common folk and their wives against their brother Jews. 'We must pawn our fields, our vineyards and our homes to get grain to stave off hunger. We have to borrow money to pay the king's tax. Nehemiah responded by saying 'it angered me very much to hear their outcry and these complaints . . . . Are you pressing claims on loans made to your brothers . . . We have done our best to buy back our Jewish brothers who were sold to nations, will you now sell your brothers so that they must be sold back to us? . . . What you are doing is not right? Give back at once their fields, their vineyards, their olive trees, and their homes.' The nobles agreed 'We shall give them back, and not demand anything from them; we shall do just as you say.' Neh 5:1-13

Nehemiah was not just a talker either. During these hard times, he shouldered the burden himself. 'Although there were at my table, between Jews and perfects, one hundred fifty men in all, I did not resort to the governor's food allowance, for the king's service lay heavily on the people.

O, my God, remember to my credit all that I have done for this people!' Neh 5:17-19

The book of Nehemiah may have been saved and cherished because he was a good governor. Indeed, where do we find men today willing to forgo what they are due in times when so many have not? Further it may have been cherished by our forefathers because as the Oxford commentators write 'One of the most striking characteristics of the memoir is a series of four formulaic prayers containing the word 'remember.'

The wall of Jerusalem had been rebuilt from the dust heap. Nehemiah and Ezra worked with the people to remember their past 'At that time they read to the people from the Book of Moses.' Neh 13:1 Nehemiah helped them reinstitute the tithe and other proper worship practices. Nehemiah also prayed for God to remember "O my God, remember me favorably for this, and do not blot out the devotion I showed toward the House of God and its attendants . . . . This too, O my God, remember to my credit, and spare me in accord with your abundant faithfulness . . . . O, my God, remember it for my credit! Neh 13:29-30

24th Sunday – Read Esther

'Who knows? Perhaps you have come for just such a time as this.' Esther 4:14

September 19, 2010

Esther – For all the Jews in Diaspora, there seemed little reason for hope. Babylonian King Nebuchadnezzar had forced all the Jews to leave their homeland. Later Persia came to power and they remained scattered all over the region. Comic relief was in order. A good story needed to be told to provide hope. Esther fit this bill. So Esther should be read as a comedy but with a serious message for the Jewish people.

The story of Ester takes place around a series of 10 drinking banquets. There is the inept Persian King Ahasuerus and his chief flunky Haman who tries to set foreign policy. Ahasuerus wants to live the good life and have all the pretty girls. Haman wants to constantly be known as the most honorable person in the king's court.

The story begins when the party goers get drunk and ask the king to call for the lovely Queen Vashti so they can ogle her. The queen wants no part of this and refuses the king's order to make an appearance at the party. At this point we get a sense of the silliness of the text. All the king's men shout "not only has Queen Vashti done wrong to the king, but to all the officials and all the peoples who are in all the provinces of King Ahasuerus.' The go on to suggest that the queen's actions will cause all women in the country to have 'contempt for their husbands . . . . there will be no end of contempt and wrath! So they had the king expel the queen and draft a letter that was sent to all the provinces allowing them to save face. "He sent letters to all the royal provinces, to every province in its own script and to every people in its own language, declaring that every man should be the master in his own house.' Esth 1:16-20 The story is quite funny.

Then there is a beauty search put on for a new queen. Here is where the story turns Jewish. We are told about a man named Mordecai whose family had become captives under the Babylonians and carried away to a distant land. Mordecai adopted his cousin Esther because her parents had died. When Mordecai read about the king's search he thought that since Esther was 'fair and beautiful' Esth 2:7 she might have a shot at becoming queen.

So Esther and seven 'chosen maidens from the king's place were chosen to see who was the most beautiful.' Mordecai admonished Esther not to reveal her Jewish identify during the competition. The ladies are sent to the finest Persian spa for 12 months 'since this was the regular period of their cosmetic treatments, six months with oil of myrrh and six months with perfumes and cosmetics for women.'

When the maidens are all gussied up, they each get a night with the king. 'When Esther was taken to King Ahasuerus . . . the king loved Esther more than all the other women . . . so he set the royal crown on her head. Then they have another big party this time in Esther's honor. Esth 2:8-18

Mordecai used to sit at the town gate and keep up with the gossip. He heard rumor that someone was trying to assassinate the king. Mordecai gets word through Esther to the king and the would be killers were hanged. Mordecai has a little standing now too.

Now this guy Haman who was king's most trusted advisor did not like that Mordecai would not 'bow down or do obeisance' Esth 3:2 like all the other king's servants. So Haman hatched a plot to have all the Jews destroyed. He said to the king 'There is a certain people scattered and separated among the peoples in all the provinces of your kingdom; their laws are different from those of every other people, and they do not keep the king's laws, so that it is not appropriate for the king to tolerate them. If it pleases the king, let a decree be issued for their destruction.' The king tells Haman 'to do with them as it seems good to you.' More letters are sent to all the provinces that on a certain date in the future, people loyal to the king are to 'destroy, to kill and to annihilate all Jews, young and old, women and children, in one day.' Esth 3:8-12

Mordecai by now we know hears of secret plots. When he finds out about this one, he gets to Esther and asks her to intervene on behalf of the Jews. But there was a problem; one couldn't just barge in on the king. 'Only if the king holds out the golden scepter to someone, may that person live.' Esth 4:11

Interestingly, there is no mention of God in book of Esther. There is some mourning and fasting but no praying. But there are huge theological overtones in the book. Probably the biggest comes when Mordecai replies to Esther's reluctance to go see the king without being invited. Mordecai says 'Do not think that in the king's palace you will escape any more than all the other Jews. For if you keep silence at such a time as this, relief and deliverance will rise for the Jews from another quarter, but you and your father's family will perish. Who knows? Perhaps you have come to royal dignity for just such a time as this.' Esth 4:14

The drama gets intense in the next few chapters. Esther boldly approaches the king. He holds out the golden cup toward her and listens to her plan to have a banquet to honor the villain Haman. The king is all for another big party.

Haman is thrilled to get this honor but he still has to walk through the palace gates everyday and see Mordecai refusing to bow down. Haman goes home that night and tells his wife about the big honor he is getting and then says 'yet all this does me no good so long as I see the Jew Mordecai sitting at the king's gate.' Esth 5:13 Haman thinks to heck with his and order's his men to build a seven story gallows intended for Mordecai.

The king was restless that night and for some reason he remembered the time when Mordecai foiled the assignation plot.

Long story short, Esther asks the king to overrule the plot to kill her people. The king asked who would destroy her people and she says 'A foe and enemy, this wicked Haman! Esth 7:6 In a dramatic reversal of fortune, Mordecai is invited to wear royal robes and Haman is hung on the gallows he had built.

The story of Ester is basis for the Jewish celebration called Purim. According to the Jewish Bible Esther, 'Does have a serious side, and an important function as a Diaspora story . . . it promotes Jewish identity, solidarity within the Jewish community, and a strong connection with Jewish (biblical) tradition . . . . Good triumphs and evil is eradicated; the threat of Jewish annihilation is averted and the Jewish community is assured of continuity and prosperity . . . . The book succeeds in putting a serious message in a comic form.'

25th Sunday – Read Job

'Jobs friends sat with him seven days; none spoke a word.' Job 2:13

September 26, 2010

Job – The book of Job is one of the most beautiful books ever written. Victor Hugo wrote, 'Tomorrow, if all literature was to be destroyed and it was left to me to retain one work only, I should save Job.' I think Job is coveted not only because of the graceful writing but also because it addresses a timeless question. That is, why do good people suffer? More poignant than the writing or the great question it addresses may be the fact that the book does not give a clear cut answer to why righteous people suffer. We are left as Roger Hahn writes to 'ponder what all the speeches and answers mean.'

Job begins in style of a good old fashion tale. 'There was a man in the land of Uz named Job. That man was blameless and upright; he feared God and shunned evil. Job was a rich man and pious to the point that he regularly prayed and made sacrifices for each one of his children. "Perhaps my children have sinned and blasphemed God in their thoughts.' Job 1:1:5 If Job were a play, soft beautiful music would be playing in the opening describing Job the perfect. But about now the music would turn dark and moody.

'One day the divine beings presented themselves before the Lord, and the Adversary came along with them.' God asked the Adversary what he had been doing. The evil one responded 'I have been roaming all over the earth.' The Lord holds up Job as one upstanding man. Satan smirks 'Does Job not have good reason to fear God? Why, it You who have fenced him round, him and his household and all that he has.' Job 1:6:-10 Evil proposes that Job would cuss God like a sailor at the first sign of bad luck. God allows the test to proceed saying the devil could do anything he wanted to Job except kill him.

The devil arranges for enemies to kill Job's sons. Storms wipe out all his holdings. Then, 'The Adversary departed from the presence of the Lord and inflicted a severe inflammation on Job from the sole of his foot to the crown of his head.' As Job itched and scratched his wife said 'You still keep your integrity! Blaspheme God and die! But Job calmly replies "Should we accept only good from God and not accept evil? Job 2:7-10

At this point we might become uncomfortable with the images of God allowing Job to be tested. The Bible is quite clear on this though. Abraham was tested. In Deuteronomy we read that the Israelites were constantly being tested 'Remember the long way that the LORD your God has led you these forty years in the wilderness, in order to humble you, testing you to know what was in your heart, whether or not you would keep his commandments.' Deut 8:2

When friends of Job hear of his trouble, they come to visit him. The only good thing the friends do is sit with him in silence for seven days. Then they begin to proffer advice. They are Eliphaz the Temanite, Bildad the Shuhite and Zophar the Maanathite. Later we also read of a fourth friend Elihu 'the intruder' who inserts himself late into the legal drama.

The premise of the prosecution is typified by Eliphaz who said, 'As I have seen, those who plow evil and sow mischief reap them.' Job 4:8 The friends go on to say that Job has neglected the poor. Job's friends think that he has had bad luck because he deserved it. After three cycles of speeches they rest their case.

But Job will not be wrongly accused. He blasts back 'On my part, I will not speak with restraint; I will give voice to the anguish of my spirit; I will complain in the bitterness of my soul.' Job 7:11

Job not only answers his counterparts but makes clear he wants a direct audience with God. 'Indeed, I would speak to the Almighty; I insist on arguing with God. But you invent lies; all of you are quacks. If you would only keep quiet it would be considered wisdom on your part.' 'Your briefs are empty platitudes; your responses are unsubstantial.' Job 13:3-12

Job continues his diatribe hoping to get a conversation started with God. 'Why do you hide your face, and treat me like and an enemy?' Job 13:24 'I cry out to You, but You do not answer me; I wait but You do not consider me.' Job 30:29

Out of the blue in chapter 38 the Lord speaks. 'Who is this that darkens counsel, speaking without knowledge? Gird your loins like a man, I will ask and you will inform Me. Where were you when I laid the earth's foundations? Speak if you have understanding Job 38:2- 4 . . . . Shall one who should be disciplined complain against Shaddai? He who arraigns God must respond. Job said in reply to the Lord: See, I am of small worth; what can I answer You? I clap my hand to my mouth. I have spoken once, and will not reply.' Job 401:4

The Lord pounds Job one last time. Job meekly replies, 'I know that You can do everything, that nothing is impossible for You. Indeed, I have spoken without understanding.' Job 42:2-3

In the finale, the Lord rebukes Job's friends, 'I am incensed at you, for you have not spoken the truth about Me as did My servant Job.' Then, 'The

Lord restored Job's fortunes when he prayed on behalf of his friends, and the Lord gave Job twice what he had before.' 42:7-10

Picking back up with an analysis of Roger Hahn, he writes, 'Throughout Jewish and Christian history Job has spoken powerful words of hope and comfort to people who have suffered or who have found faith difficult. For people who are not satisfied with simple answers Job rings a word of truth.'

Hahn concludes that the real message of Job is not really about suffering but 'why the righteous serve God.' Robert Sutherland takes this further when he writes; it is common to suggest that the purpose of the book is to answer the age-old question, 'Why does God allow the righteous to suffer?' 'But it is worthy to note that Job never receives a direct answer.' 'Therefore, I suggest the purpose of the book is to answer the question, 'How should the righteous suffer.'

For me, I would add that we could learn from Job's friends too. Instead of offering advice or wisdom to people who suffer, we should just sit with them in silence.

26th Sunday – Read Psalms

'Hide me in the shadow of thy wings.' Psalm 17:18

October 3, 2010

Psalms – What makes the Psalms so special? Consider Chilean miner Ricardo Villaroel who was literally in the pit. "I felt fear', he said after the mine collapsed. 'We had a boss . . . everyday he would tell us we had to be strong and they ask us . . . we didn't have hope. Strength comes from internal energy and prayer . . . I never used to pray, here I learned to pray. I got closer to God.'

Walter Brueggemann in 'Praying the Psalms' says the Psalms 'are the voice of our own common humanity-gathered over a long period of time . . . And so when we turn to the Psalms it means we enter into the middle of humanity and decide to take our stand with that voice.... The Psalter knows that life is dislocated. There need be no cover-up. The Psalter is a collection ... of the eloquent, passionate songs and prayers of people who are at the desperate edge of their lives.' Like Villaroel was until Thursday.

And while the Psalms 'belong to Israel,' Roland Murphy in 'The Gift of the Psalms' says the Psalms are 'Israel's gift to us.' Murphy notes that to fully appreciate the Psalms we need to know our Bibles and the imagery presented in the Psalms. He asked us to consider, 'How did the ancients, over a period of ten centuries, view reality: the world, the makeup of humans, suffering, sinfulness, and so forth" What are the concrete institutions and ideas that played a role in Israel's life: Covenant, Temple, Zion, Messianism.' We can further benefit our reading by having a working knowledge of the different types of Psalms. Generally, they are categorized as praise, thanksgiving or lament.

A typical example of a praise hymn is Psalm 8 which begins and ends with 'O Lord, our Sovereign, how majestic is your name in all the earth!' We can read about thanksgiving in Psalm 124 'If it had not been the Lord was on our side, let Israel now say- if it had not been the Lord who was on our side, when men rose against us, then they would have swallowed us up alive ... ' The lament is famously exemplified by Psalm 22, 'My God, my God, why have you forsaken me? Why are you so far from helping me, from the words of my groaning? O my God, I cry by day, but you do not answer; and by night, but find no rest.' (Jesus knew his Hebrew scriptures).

But it seems to me that we moderns just really want to tip toe around with our faith. We like singing uplifting songs of praise. We like giving thanks to God when we get that promotion or a negative report on a medical test. But the ancients let it all hang out to God. They didn't want to get in the pit. And when they did get in it, they wanted God to help get them out. Brueggemann says in his book that 'the pit refers to the experience of being rendered powerless.' For example in Psalm 69 we read, 'Do not let the flood sweep over me, or the deep swallow me up, or the Pit close its mouth over me.'

We don't want to be in the pit either. What we want according to Brueggemann is to be 'safe under the protective wings of God.' Whereas the pit speaks of danger and threat, wings speak of safety, tenderness and nurture.' Psalm 17:8 'Keep me as the apple of thy eye; hide me in the shadow of thy wings.' Brueggemann concludes by saying 'Our lives move between the pit and the wing, between the shattering disorientation and the gift of life . . . . It is clear that the Psalms, when we freely engage in them, are indeed subversive literature. They break things loose. They disrupt and question. Most of all, they give us new eyes to see and new tongues to speak. And therefore, we need not enter the Presence of the Holy One mute and immobilized.'

So to reconnect with my earlier thought about not minding praise or thanksgiving, we might have trouble with some of the Psalms when we read about violence or wishing harm upon on people. A good example of this might be, Psalm 139:19, 21-22 'O that you would kill the wicked, O God, and that the bloodthirsty would depart from me—Do I not hate those who hate you, O Lord? And do I not loathe those who rise up against you? I hate them with perfect hatred; I count them my enemies.'

Murphy says that we need to come to terms with this type of Psalm. 'These Psalms challenge us to think and to meditate; they cannot scandalize.' He encourages us to 'hear the word! Hear the agony and even the sinful violence of human beings- in the context of prayer. These expressions of rage exemplify the demonic in every human heart. No one is exempt from feelings of revenge. When they are heard in prayer, they serve first to illumine and then perhaps even convict our own feelings.' Murphy goes on to say that we can bypass the lament Psalms or the passages. 'But bypassing does not mean dismissing. Rather, we address the violence, mediate on it, and weigh realistically the surges of violence and vengeance that permeate our daily existence. We confront human sinfulness and take a stand.'

And so we read the Psalms to take a stand, a stand that distinguishes us as a people with hope. With few exceptions, the underlying attitude of the Psalter, after all the adoration and all the tears and all the rage, is hopeful. See Psalm 27:13-14, 'I believe that I shall see the goodness of the Lord in the land of the living. Wait for the Lord; be strong, and let your heart take courage; wait for the Lord!' Or Psalm 62:5 "For God alone my soul waits in silence, for my hope is from Him.'

I often read writing by a preacher named Dr James Howell who knew the Roland Murphy I quoted above. Howell says that Murphy was 'A brilliant, wise teacher, he believed every Christian should read (or rather, pray) the

Psalms in a disciplined way: one in the morning, and one in the evening, from Psalm 1 through Psalm 150, and then do it again, and again – as he did from his teenage years until his death at age 85.'

Let us then read aloud and pray the Psalms together. From Psalm 33:

'The Lord looks down from heaven; he sees all humankind. From where he sits enthroned he watches all the inhabitants of the earth— he who fashions the hearts of them all, and observes all their deeds. A king is not saved by his great army; a warrior is not delivered by his great strength. The war horse is a vain hope for victory, and by its great might it cannot save. Truly the eye of the Lord is on those who fear him, on those who hope in his steadfast love, to deliver their soul from death, and to keep them alive in famine. Our soul waits for the Lord; he is our help and shield. Our heart is glad in him, because we trust in his holy name. Let your steadfast love, O Lord, be upon us, even as we hope in you.' Amen.

27th Sunday – Read Proverbs

'A cheerful look brings joy to the heart, and good news health to the bones.' Prov 17:22

October 10, 2010

Proverbs – Where do we find wisdom in our society today? We hear people shout over each other on the television news. Political opponents resort to vile personal attacks instead of debating on the issues. Parents of children playing sports scream at the kids, coaches and referees as though Olympic gold medals were on the line. Words are cast about too loosely. Roland Murphy in 'The Tree of Life' says 'the topic of speech deserves special attention. After all, words are the coin of the wisdom realm.'

Proverbs then is a book of words about wisdom. The wisdom books of the Bible (Proverbs, Job and Ecclesiastes; Sirach and The Wisdom of Solomon if you count the Apocrypha) don't get a lot of mention from the pulpit today (perhaps because there are no Israel stories in them). This is sad because 'Wisdom is a tree of life to those who lay hold of her; fortunate are they who embrace her; those who lay hold of her will be blessed. Proverbs 3:18.' Murphy goes on the say that wisdom is described in a lot of different ways. 'She is 'fear of the Lord, instruction for moral formation, human experience, the mysteries of creation, Law or Torah, a mysterious divine call, and even a spouse.' To strive for wisdom Murphy notes that we 'must hear Wisdom obediently' and 'pray for the gift that she is.'

The proverbs aim to tell about how life really is. 'As the crucible tests silver and the furnace gold, so one is tested by the praise he receives Proverbs 27:21.' 'For the lips of an adulteress drip honey, and her speech is smoother than oil, but in the end she is bitter as gall, sharp as a double-edged sword. Proverbs 5:4-5'

The Proverbs are just little signets or poems. When we read them, if they seem to simple or commonsensical we may not have reflected on them enough. Ellen Davis in her Westminster Bible Companion commentary says the Proverbs need to be read slowly. The proverbs among other wisdom literature 'demands that we read it a little bit at a time, even verse-by-verse, paying close attention to the particular words and the form of the poem, and at the same time letting our minds move freely to follow the association they suggest. Especially important . . . is pondering the significance of echoes we hear from other parts of the Bible.' 'The one who oppresses the poor insults his Maker, but one who is kind to the needy honors Him. Proverbs 14:3.'

Roland Murphy points out that God intended for us to seek wisdom that we might have a good and fruitful life. He points out 'a remarkable passage' about the origins of Lady Wisdom. 'The Lord brought me forth as the first of his works, I was appointed from eternity, from the beginning, before the world began Proverbs 8:22-23.'

The foe of Lady Wisdom is Dame Folly. 'The woman Folly is loud; she is undisciplined and without knowledge . . . . Let all who are simple come in here! She says to those who lack judgment, Stolen water is sweet; food eaten in secret is delicious! But little do they know that the dead are there, that her guests are in the depths of the grave.' Proverbs 9:13-18.

Folly seems to be the leader of modern day and this reminds me of my original question. Where do we find wisdom? Davis points out that the ancients placed high value on learning wisdom. In contrast she writes, 'In Western society, we have followed the Greek preference for analytical prose writing, that is, for philosophy and, above all in the last three centuries, science.' Further she adds gone is ' . . . the traditional idea that learning from our elders and our ancestors is essential to living a decent and contended life. On the contrary, traditional views are often suspect; they are regarded as out of touch with human needs, even oppressive. In a culture that has flattered itself into believing that we are inventing a new way of living, a new way of being human, the idea of trusting our predecessors to provide guidance can only seem foolish.'

Both Murphy and Davis spend time in their commentaries writing about how wisdom evolved. Over many centuries the wisest of our oldest (sages) paid attention to what worked and what didn't work in the family / tribe units. Murphy notes that 'The home may be regarded as perhaps the original site of wisdom teaching before and after such teaching became professionalized among the sages . . . The implication of all this is that the origins of wisdom thought are to be sought in the family and tribe rather than in any kind of school associated with court and temple.' More on this in a moment.

Still the sages understood that God created a good world and He created a certain order for things. Not only the rotation of the planets but how humans should live. Davis writes that' human wisdom consists in observing the created order, learning from it, living in its ways that do not violate- indeed, that contribute- to the well-being of the whole created order.' Where do we find this sort of thought process in the 'Me' generation?

Now here is some commentary of my own. The family is breaking down in our country and our society is disintegrating as a result. What is the problem? I think we lack wisdom. Men and women need to get married before they have children and then stay married. Families need to spend time at the dinner table together. Families need to go to church midweek and then again on Sunday morning. Families also need to read great wisdom literature and discuss it in the home. I heard someone say that all the fuss about taking down the Ten Commandments from schools and courthouses is a ruse. That is, because if we were teaching and living these commands at home, we wouldn't worry about having them enshrined in public places. We need to spend less time being entertained and more time getting wise.

Abraham Joshua Heschel wrote, 'Ask the average man; what are your goals in life? He'll tell you: Life insurance, a Cadillac, and a color television.' Heschel encourages us to teach our young people that 'There is meaning beyond all the absurdity. Let them be sure that every deed counts, that every word has power, and that we can, everyone, do our share to redeem the world' And he says we do this through self-discipline and by studying the sources of wisdom.

A closing fountain of wisdom: When pride comes, then comes disgrace, but with humility comes wisdom 11:12 . . . wealth is worthless in the day of wrath but righteousness delivers from death 11:4 . . . reckless words pierce like a sword, but the tongue of the wise brings healing 12:8. . . . The leech has two daughters, Give! Give! They cry 30:15 . . . . A cheerful look brings joy to the heart, and good news health to the bones.' 17:22 Thank you sages!

28th Sunday – Read Ecclesiastes

'Who can make straight what He has made crooked?'

October 17, 2010

Ecclesiastes – Earlier this week while reading Ecclesiastes with one eye and watching a Seinfeld rerun with the other, I thought that George Costanza could be a modern day Koheleth. Koheleth is the naysayer who wrote the book of Ecclesiastes. In the Seinfeld episode called 'The Statute', George laments that his mother's figurine had been stolen:

GEORGE: Ma, will you stop? It's just a statue! How is it my fault?! . . . It was stolen. I didn't even touch it this time . . . Okay, fine . . . She doesn't react to disappointment very well. Unlike me.

GEORGE: There's just no justice. This experience has changed me. It's made me more cynical, more bitter, more jaded.

Ecclesiastes is an odd book by biblical standards. It's cynical and jaded towards the negative. But because it is catalogued with the 'Wisdom' books of the Bible perhaps it needs to be examined more carefully than a casual read might prompt one to do.

Koheleth is confounded. First, he lifts up the superiority of wisdom:

"My thoughts turned to appraising wisdom and madness and folly. I found that wisdom is superior to folly, as light is superior to darkness; A wise man has his eyes in his head, whereas a fool walks in darkness.' Ecc 2:13-14

But then Koheleth puts the kibosh to this line of thinking by adding:

"But I also realized that the same fate awaits them both. So I reflected 'The fate of the fool is also destined for me; to what advantage, then, have I been wise? 'Because the wise man, just like the fool, is not remembered forever; as the succeeding days roll by, both are forgotten. Alas, the wise man dies, just like the fool!' Ecc 2:15-16

Roland Murphy in 'Tree of Life' calls Koheleth a skeptic. Koheleth thinks that everything is futile so all there is left to do is enjoy life. Murphy says 'The reader should be ready, therefore, for the tensions within the book and to keep them in careful balance.'

'Utter futility!-said Koheleth- Utter futility! All is futile! What real value is there for a man in all the gains he makes beneath the sun!' Ecc 1:2

In the introduction of her Westminster Bible Companion commentary, Ellen Davis cites Ellie Wiesel as saying 'True faith lies beyond questions; true faith comes after it has been challenged.' Davis goes on to say that Ecclesiastes 'highlights every absurdity in human experience, every contradiction in human thought . . . it seems to me that the teaching of

Proverbs is an exercise, which trains our souls and makes them supple for the struggle with Ecclesiastes.'

Koheleth 'is no mere cynic, content to strip us of illusions and leave us bare. Rather, his nay-saying is the means by which he conveys essential religious instruction and carves out his own niche with the canon of scripture . . . Koheleth teaches more concretely than any other biblical book about humility. And the core of his teaching on humility is this: life can never be mastered or shaped in conformity with our desires. It can only be enjoyed, when pleasures great or small come our way, or, when enjoyment is not possible, it must be endured.'

Davis says that 'Koheleth is reflecting on the great questions that occupy thinkers of every generation; the meaning of life, the unfairness of fate; the inevitability of death-but more, death's cruelty in stripping us of all dignity, distinctiveness, achievement. His mind is restless, subtle, and unable to accept any answers, even his own . . . Koheleth chooses an unsettled style that imitates life itself. . . . He keeps returning to his basic themes –work, money, pleasure, power, wisdom, death, God-yet he never gives a lengthy statement on any of them. Moreover, he seems not to mind if he contradicts himself in the process.'

Davis points out Koheleth is constantly using the Hebrew word 'hevel' (vanity, futility) to convey the nuanced feelings of absurdity / emptiness in understanding the 'disparity between what we plan for and what actually happens.' She concludes that 'a key thing we can learn from Koheleth is a reminder about the brevity of human life . . . thus the very fact that life is passing away exposes the absurdity of certain human behaviors-unfortunately, behaviors that are very common among us all.'

Ecclesiastes is an odd book that's for sure. But Murphy notes that the 'ancients . . . .were not as 'shocked' as modern readers are who consider Koheleth to be in revolt against everything in the tradition. Yes, his was a deeply critical an even strident voice that did not sing in tune with the others; but the ancients made room for him among the sages.'

It has been my observation that many modern day Bible bullet readers / cheerleaders never seem to get down on their knees in agony over all the misery and inconsistencies in life. Koheleth didn't let the overly pious of his generation off the hook. 'Just as you do not know how the breath comes to the bones in the mother's womb, so you do not know the work of God, who makes everything. Ecc 11:5

Robert Asa wrote that one view of Ecclesiastes 'as a whole may be seen as the voice of theological rebuke to the religiously naïve who overlook the discrepancies between their sunny faith and the hard facts of life. If faith avoids hard questions rather than asks them, it is not faith but credulity.'

'And I have observed all that God brings to pass. Indeed, man cannot guess the events that occur under the sun. For man tires strenuously, but fails to guess them; and even if a sage should think to discover them he would not be able to guess them.' Ecc 8:17

'Who can make straight what He has made crooked? Ecc 7:13

Therefore,

Go, eat your bread in gladness, and drink your wine in joy, for your action was long ago approved by God.' Ecc 9:7

29th Sunday – Read Song of Songs

'Strengthen me with raisins; refresh me with apples, for I am faint with love.'

October 24, 2010

Song of Songs – Why is erotic love poetry in the Bible?

'Let him kiss me with the kisses of his mouth- for your love is more delightful than wine.

Pleasing is the fragrance of your perfumes; your name is like perfume poured out.

No wonder the maidens love you!

Take me away with you-let us hurry! Let the king bring me into his chambers.' Songs 1:1-4

Many think that the book is just a love poem. Others go to the opposite extreme of making every word and phrase allegory. The Jewish sages made room for the skeptic Koheleth and they also made room for a grand poem about love. So what does it mean?

Rabbi Louis Jacobs wrote about the Song of Songs in an article titled 'All the writings are holy; but Song of Songs is the Holy of Holies.'

Jacobs says 'the Rabbis in the second century CE could debate whether the Song of Songs belongs to the sacred Scripture is evidence enough that in this period there were some who took it all literally as a dialogue of love between a man and a woman, sexual desire expressed exquisitely but the with utmost frankness.'

Recent Jewish commentary says it 'can still be sacred literature, since love between husband and wife is holy and divinely ordained . . . But the standard Rabbinic view and the reason why Rabbi Akiba declared the book to be the 'Holy of Holies' is that the Rabbi's saw the 'lover' as God and the beloved as the community of Israel.'

Jacobs continues, 'The sixteen-century mystic, Moses Cordovero, interprets the book as a dialogue between the individual soul and God. What is the proper form of the love of God? It is that he should love the Lord with great, overpowering, fierce love to the extent that his soul is bound to the love of God and he dwells on it constantly, as if he were love-sick for a woman and dwells on this constantly, whether in sitting or standing, eating or drinking.'

'Strengthen me with raisins; refresh me with apples, for I am faint with love. Songs 2:5

'Love the Lord with all your heart and with all your soul and with all your strength.' Deut 6:5

Ellen Davis in her WBC commentary notes 'There is in the whole book not a single overt reference to God, to prayer, or to any aspect of Israel's religious practice or tradition.' She writes that 'modern commentators tend adhere rigidly to a sexual interpretation, decoding the highly metaphorical language of the Song into a series of physically explicit references. The suggestion that religious experience is part of what the poet had in mind is regarded as foreign, if not hostile, to the Song's celebration of faithful human love.'

But Davis counters that we need to be reminded about love without promise of material gain. 'The experience of healthy sexual desire can help us imagine what it might mean to love God truly- a less natural feeling for many of us, especially in our secular society. On the other hand, from what the Bible tells us about God's love we can come to recognize sexual love as an arena for the formation of the soul. Like the love of God, profound love of another person entails devotion of the whole self and steady practice of repentance and forgiveness, it inevitably requires of us suffering and sacrifice . . . . So the Song affirms that the desire for loving intimacy both in sexual relationship and in relationship with God is fundamental to our humanity.'

'My beloved in mine and I am his.' Song 2:16

And the Song ends:

Come away, my lover, and be like a gazelle or like a young stag on the spice-laden mountains.' Song 8:14

30th Sunday – Read Isaiah

'Ha! You who hide a plan too deep for the Lord, whose deeds are in the dark, and who say, 'Who sees us? Who knows us?' Isa 29:15

October 31, 2010

Isaiah – In his book 'The Prophets' Abraham Joshua Heschel wrote that the prophets are 'some of the most disturbing people who have ever lived.' Heschel goes on to say 'The prophet was an individual who said No to society, condemning its habits and assumptions, its complacency, waywardness, and syncretism . . . His fundamental objective was to reconcile man and God. Why do the two need reconciliation? Perhaps it is due to man's false sense of sovereignty, to his abuse of freedom, to his aggressive, sprawling pride, resenting God's involvement in history.'

Heschel says we need to understand the prophet sees all injustice as disaster. 'They speak and act as if the sky were about to collapse because Israel has become unfaithful to God . . . the rebuke is harsh and relentless . . . A prophet is a man who feels fiercely. God has thrust a burden upon his soul, and he is bowed and stunned at man's fierce greed.'

'The prophet's word is a scream in the night. While the world is at ease and asleep, the prophet feels the blast from heaven.' 'In his words, the invisible God becomes visible.' Dire though is not the only word. The prophet 'begins with a message of doom; he concludes with a message of hope.'

Enter the first major prophet Isaiah. Isaiah lays out his case right from the beginning.

'Oh sinful nation, a people loaded with guilt, a brood of evildoers, children given to corruption! They have forsaken the Lord; they have spurned the Holy One of Israel and turned their backs on him.' Isa 1:4

'The multitude of your sacrifices-what are they to me? says the Lord . . . Stop bringing meaningless offerings! They have become a burden to me.' Isa 1:11

'Take your evil deeds out of my sight! Stop doing wrong, learn to do right! Seek justice, encourage the oppressed, defend the cause of the fatherless, plead the cause of the widow.' Isa 1:17

'Come now, let us reason together, says the Lord. Though your sins are like scarlet, they shall be white as snow. Isa 1:18

Isaiah is called by God to be a thorn to the tribe of Judah. Isaiah possesses the two traits which God most seeks from His followers, humility and willingness. 'Woe to me! I cried, 'I am ruined!' 'For I am a man of unclean lips, and I live among a people of unclean lips, and my eyes have seen the King, the Lord Almighty.' Isa 6:5

Then I heard the voice of the Lord saying, 'Whom shall I send? And who will god for us!' And I said, 'Here I am. Send me!' He said, 'God and tell the people.' Isa 6:8

'If you do not stand firm in your faith, you will not stand at all.' Isa 7:9

Will there be disaster! Is there any hope for the future? For the Judah to whom Isaiah writes the answer is no. 'Therefore, the Lord himself will give you a sign: The virgin will be with child and will give birth to a son, and will call him Immanuel. But before the boy knows enough to reject the wrong and choose the right, the land of the two kings you dread will be laid waste.'

To Jews and Christians of the future the answer is yes. 'but in the future he will honor Galilee of the Gentiles, by the way of the sea, along the Jordan –

The people walking in darkness have seen a great light . . . For to us a child is born, to us a son is given, and the government will be on his shoulders. And he will be called Wonderful Counselor, Mighty God, Everlasting Father, Prince of Peace . . . . He will reign on David's throne and over his kingdom, establishing and upholding it with justice and righteousness from that time on and forever. The zeal of the Lord Almighty will accomplish this.' Isa 9:1-6

In the meantime, as Heschel writes 'The poor, oppressed, helpless people are waiting for God to deliver them.'

For 66 chapters Isaiah alternates between his message of doom and his message of hope. One minute he is blasting us for being dull and not hearing. He is chastising us for the lack of injustice on the earth. Isaiah proclaims that we humans have turned things upside down. God is the potter and we are the clay. God is sorrowful for the conditions on earth. The next minute the prophet tells us God wants to be our friend. God calls Israel and us: 'A precious vineyard—sing to it! I, the Lord, am its keeper; every moment I water it.' Isa 27:2-3

Heschel says that we need to hear the message in the beginning of the book about our noisy worship and realize 'that the primary way of serving God is through love, justice and righteousness . . . . righteousness is not just a value; it is God's part of human life, God's stake in human history.'

God's justice is more than we think. Heschel writes "Justice was not equal justice, but a bias in favor of the poor.'

'Seek justice,
Undo oppression;
Defend the fatherless;
Plead of the widow.'

Isaiah is not just writing to ancient Israel. He is writing to me and you and about the future. But we need to feel the prophet's blast from heaven and be moved to:

'Give thanks to the Lord,
Call upon his name,
Make his deeds known among the nations,
Proclaim that His name is exalted,
Sing praises to the Lord . . .
Shout, sing for joy . . .
For great in your midst is the Holy One of Israel.' Isa 12:4-6

31st Sunday – Read Jeremiah

'Let him who glories, glory in this.' Jer 9:24

November 7, 2010

Jeremiah – The Jewish study Bible lays the framework for reading this book: 'Jeremiah lived during one of most crucial and terrifying periods in the history of the Jewish people in biblical times: the destruction of Jerusalem and the Temple of Solomon followed by the beginning of the Babylonian exile.'

The book begins:

'The word of the Lord came to me.'

'Before I created you in the womb, I selected you; before you were born, I consecrated you; I appointed you a prophet concerning the nations. Jer 1:4

Jeremiah replies in the humble fashion we are accustomed to this far into the Bible.

'Ah, Lord God!
I don't know how to speak,
For I am still a child.
And the Lord said to me:
Do not say, I am still child
But go wherever I command you.' Jer 1:6-8

The Northern Kingdom of Israel had perished. Jeremiah speaks to the remaining tribe of Judah:

'The Lord said to me in the days of King Josiah: Have you seen what Rebel Israel did, going after every high mountain and under every tree, and whoring there? Rebel Israel was destroyed. Still seeing this, Faithless Judah was not afraid- she too went and whored.' Jer 3:6

Heschel in the Prophets writes 'The pages of the prophetic writings are filled with echoes of divine love and disappointment, mercy and indignation. The God of Israel is never impersonal.'

'Return, faithless Israel, says the Lord, I will not look on you in anger, for I am merciful, says the Lord.' 3:12

Jeremiah was troubled and tried to make sense of the devastation and destruction about to unfold.

Oh, my suffering, my suffering! How I writhe!
Oh, the walls of my heart!
My heart moans within me, I cannot be silent.' Jer 4:19

Jeremiah had visions:

'Lo, I am bringing against you, O House of Israel a nation from afar- declares the Lord. A nation whose language you do not know . . . will devour your harvest and food, your sons and daughters, flocks and herds, vines and fig trees. They will batter down with the sword the fortified towns on which you rely.' Jer 5:15-16

Jeremiah tried to get the people to change course and preached mightily in chapters 7 – 10.

'Don't put your trust in illusions and say, The Temple of the Lord, the Temple of the Lord, the Temple of the Lord, these are just buildings.' Jer 7:4

'No if you really mend your ways and your actions, if you execute justice between one man and another, if you do not oppress the stranger, the orphan, and the widow, if you do not shed the blood of the innocent in this place, if you do not follow other gods, to your own hurt – then only will I let you dwell in this place, in the land I gave to your fathers for all time.' Jer 7:5-7

If not, then 'I will turn Jerusalem into rubble, into dens for jackals, and I will make the towns of Judah desolation without inhabitants.' Jer 9:11

What man is so wise that he understands this?' Jer 9:12

'Thus says the Lord, let not the wise man glory in his wisdom,
Let not the strong man glory in his strength;
Let not the rich man glory in his riches.
But let him who glories, glory in this,
that he understands and knows me,
that I am the Lord who practices steadfast love, justice and righteousness in the world;
For in these things I delight, says the Lord.' 9:23-24

'Hark a noise! It is coming, a great commotion out of the north,
That the towns of Judah may be made desolation, a haunt of jackals.' Jer 10:22

'Proclaim all these things through the towns of Judah: Hear the terms of the covenant and perform them,. For I have repeatedly and persistently warned your fathers from the time I brought them out of Egypt to this day saying: Obey My Commands. But they did not listen or give ear. They all followed the willfulness of their evil hearts.' Jer 11:1-9

Jeremiah argues with God trying to figure it all out: 'You will win, O Lord if I make a claim against you: But why does the way of the wicked prosper? How long must the land languish and the grass in all the countryside be dried up.' Jer 12:1-4

The Lord responds "I will take them back into favor and restore the each to his own inheritance and his own land if they learn the ways of my people.' Jer 16:14

Heschel writes 'Man is unable to redeem himself, to cure the sickness of the heart. What hurts the soul, the soul adores. Can man be remade? A prophet can give man a new word, but not a new heart. It is God who must give man a heart to know that He is God.'

'I will give them a heart to know me that I am the Lord.' Jer 24:7

For I know the plans I have for you, declares the Lord. Plans to prosper you and not to harm you, plans to give you a future. Then you will call upon me and come and pray to me, and I will listen to you. You will seek me and find me when you seek me with all your heart. I will be found by you declares the Lord and will bring you back from captivity.' Jer 29:11-14

God's people in exile will not be forsaken forever.

'Call to me and I will answer you and tell you great and unsearchable things you do not know.' Jer 33:3

The prophet brings the word: 'The days are coming, declares the Lord, when I will fulfill the gracious promises I made to the house of Israel and to the house of Judah.' Jer 31:1

'I have loved you with everlasting love-kindness; I will build you up again.' Jer 31:3

'The time is coming declares the Lord when I will make a new covenant with the house of Israel . . . I will put my law in their minds and write it on their hearts. I will be their God, and the will be my people.' Jer 31:31, 33

'In those days and at that time I will make a righteous Branch sprout from David's line; he will do what is just and right in the land . . . This is the name by which it will be called: The Lord Our Righteousness.' Jer 33:15-16

Jerusalem in the meantime had to fall. Heschel 'Nebuchadnezzar's soldiers burned the temple, the king's palace, the larger houses of Jerusalem. The walls were razed, most of the inhabitants deported. The Jerusalem man is busy destroying, God is erecting.'

And so it was, and so it is.

32nd Sunday – Read Lamentations

'For men are not cast off by the Lord forever. Though he brings grief, he will show compassion so great is his unfailing love.' Lam 3:32

November 14, 2010

Lamentations – Alas - All evidence points to the book being written soon after the destruction of Jerusalem and the temple in 586 BCE. The book is comprised of 5 chapters each its own poem.

J.D Cohen calls Lamentations 'the eternal lament for all Jewish catastrophes, past, present and future.' In July or August each year depending on the calendar, the Jewish community recites Lamentations in a commemoration known as the 9th of Av. Parts of the book are also recited in some Christian Good Friday services.

The primary theology put forth in the book is that the devastation suffered by the Jewish people including the destruction of the temple was God's punishment for the sins of Israel.

Daniel Grossberg in the Jewish study Bible writes 'It is God who is responsible for the destruction. Nowhere is there any doubt about the power of God, and it is this power, and also His mercy, that the poets call on for help in their present plight. But the end of Judah's suffering seems far away for most of the book. The emphasis is on the grief and suffering of the present.'

The imagery used in Lamentations helped the Jewish people work out their pain. Judah is compared to a shamed woman in the first chapter.

'Alas! Lonely sits the city once great with people! Bitterly she weeps in the night, her cheek wet with tears. There is none to comfort her of all her friends. Lam 1:1-2

The most chilling image for me in the first chapter is the utter state of loneliness. The words 'none to comfort' appears five times in the first chapter Lam 1: 2, 9, 16, 17, 21

'She is utterly disconsolate! Her enemies are now her masters, her foes are at ease, because the Lord has afflicted her for her many transgressions.' Lam1:5

'Her uncleanness clings to her skirts. She gave no thought to her future; she has sunk appallingly, with none to comfort her.' Lam 1:9

'May it never befall you, all who pass along the road. Look about and see: Is there agony like mine, which was dealt out to me when the Lord afflicted me on His day of wrath!' Lam 1:12

The second chapter describes the destruction of the city and ravaged state of its occupants.

'The Lord has acted like a foe, He has laid waste Israel, laid waste all her citadels, destroyed her strongholds.' Lam 2:5

'My eyes are spent with tears, my heart is in tumult, my being melts away over the ruin of my poor people, as babes and suckling's languish in the squares of the city.' Lam 2:11

On the day of the wrath of the Lord, none survived or escaped; those whom I bore and reared my foe has consumed.' Lam 2:22

Norman Gottwald describes the third voice in the book as declaring 'suffering in the form of an individual lament.'

'I am a man who has known affliction under the rod of His wrath.' Lam 3:1 'He has worn away by flesh and skin; He has shattered my bones. All around me he has built misery and hardship.' Lam 3:4-5

'He has broke my teeth on gravel, he has ground me into the dust . . . I forgot what happiness was.' Lam 3:16

Right in the midst of the terrible lament we have a remarkable glimpse of grace.

'But this do I call to mind, therefore I have hope; the kindness of the Lord has not ended, His mercies are not spent. They are renewed every morning- Ample is Your grace! The Lord is my portion, I say with full heart; therefore I will hope in Him.' Lam 3;21-24

The last two chapters might be seen as the collective voice of a shattered community.

'The precious children of Zion, once valued as gold-Alas, they are accounted as earthen pots . . . The tongue of the suckling cleaves to its palate for thirst! Little children beg for bread; none gives them a morsel.' Lam 4:2

The last chapter needs little clarification. It begins and ends this way:

'Remember, O Lord what has befallen us; behold, and see our disgrace!
Lam 5:1

'Unless you have utterly rejected us and are angry with us beyond measure.'
Lam 5:22

33rd Sunday – Read Ezekiel

'A new heart I will give you and a new spirit I will put within you; and I will remove from your body the heart of stone.' Ezek 11:19

November 21, 2010

Ezekiel – As I sat here this week alone with my thoughts and the words of Ezekiel it became clear to me that the prophets were speaking to more than just the ancient Israelites. They were speaking to us today. Consider the debate on religion this week between Former British Prime Minister Tony Blair and renowned atheist Christopher Hitchens.

Blair's main argument in the debate was that while bad things have certainly been done in the name of religion over the years, 'It is also undoubtedly true that people do acts of extraordinary common good inspired by religion."

Hitchens is his antagonistic style wryly rebutted by saying, 'It was not necessary to have divine permission to know right from wrong". He continued: "Religion forces nice people to do unkind things, and also makes intelligent people say stupid things."

What Hitchens promotes is a lie! Savvy to Bible bullets and religious news, Hitchens suggested an evil church that would not allow followers to use condemns was responsible for the spread of AIDS. Not a single mention of the gift of human sexuality and the responsibility and privilege to uphold a standard of decency in this arena. Just pass out condoms because people are going to have sex anyway.

But the authentic biblical voice can't be heard above the din of the crowd as Blair quietly asserts, "This is a spiritual presence, bigger, more important, more meaningful than just us alone, that has its own power separate from our power, and that even as the world's marvels multiply, makes us kneel in humility not swagger in pride.'

Some people think the prophets were just plain crazy. Heschel writes in the prophets that Hosea, Isaiah Jeremiah and Ezekiel were thought by some to be ecstatics:

For example: 'When the spirit overcame them, the prophets experienced facial contortions, their breath failed them, and occasionally they fell to the ground unconscious, for a time deprived of vision and speech and writhing in cramps.' And Heschel notes that Isaiah walked naked and barefoot for three years (Isaiah 20:3)

Looking at Isaiah walking uncovered, Heschel says there are two ways to interpret this episode. 'Isaiah going exposed about the streets of Jerusalem is a clear case of exhibitionism, a tendency which may be observed at any bathing beach, or track meet. According to another view, we have here an act of complete submission under the will of the Lord. 'The prophet threw his whole self into his prophecy, and made not his lips alone, but his whole personality, the vehicle of the divine word.'

Ezekiel then is ecstatic with vision:

'Thus says the Lord God: Clap your hands and stamp your foot, and say; Alas for all the vile abominations of the house of Israel!' Ezk 6:11 'Mortal, do you see what they are doing, the great abominations that the house of Israel are committing here to drive me out of my sanctuary?' Esk8:6

What are all the vile abominations that Ezekiel is speaking about? 'Mortal, these men have taken their idols into their hearts, and placed their iniquity as a stumbling block before them.' Ezk 14:3

God to Israel: 'Know that all lives are mine.' Ezk 18:4 (This clearly infers present and future lives.)

In Chapter 18 we have the blast from God to us about living in His ways. Which includes being, 'Righteous and lawful . . . . not defiling our neighbors wife . . . . not oppressing anyone . . . restoring to the debtor his pledge . . . committing no robbery . . . giving bread to the hungry . . . . covering the naked with a garment . . . . not taking advance or accrued interest, withholding one's hand from iniquity . . . executing true justice between contending parties . . . following God's statues and being careful to observe God's ordinances, acting faithfully- such a one is righteous.' He shall live. One who does not shall die.

Ezekiel demands, 'Repent and turn from all your transgressions; otherwise iniquity will be your ruin. Cast away from you all the transgressions that you have committed against me, and get yourselves a new heart and a new spirit! Why will you die O house of Israel? For I have no pleasure in the death of anyone, says the Lord God, Turn, then and live.' Ezk 18:30-32

We pretend to be righteous but the prophet knows better. We live for ourselves and practice idolatry with our heart, our mind, our money, and our time. Thus says the Lord, 'Know that all lives are mine.' Ezk 18:4

Bruggemann in 'OT Theology' says that idolatry is the 'wrong discernment and practice of God, the disregard of God's holiness . . . In practice idolatry (hatred of one true God) comes down to oppression (hatred of neighbor) . . . . the prophets insist that all of Israel's life is to be lived in relation to and in response to Yahweh's will and purposes . . . else 'Israel would disappear and life would be handed over, without protest, to the brutalizing, oppressive ways of life known elsewhere, rooted in the worship of wrongly discerned gods.' (Woods, Sanford, Spitzer, me, you).

'Yet you say 'The way of the Lord is unfair,' Hear now, O Israel: is my way unfair? Is in not your ways that are unfair?' Ezk 18:25

Ezekiel encountered the Glory of the Lord.

'When I saw it, I fell on my face' Mortal, I am sending you to the people of Israel, to a nation of rebels who have rebelled against me they and their ancestors have transgressed against me to this very day. The descendants were impudent and stubborn.' Ezk 2:3-4

He said to me, O mortal eat this scroll and go speak to the house of Israel. Then I ate it and in my mouth it was a sweet as honey.' Ezk 3:1-3

'Then the spirit lifted me up, and as the glory of the Lord of the Lord rose from its place . . . The spirit lifted me up and bore me away . . . . And I sat there among them, stunned for seven days.' Ezk 3:12-14

Alas, the voice of the Lord through the prophet can't be heard above the din of the crowd.

'Then the glory of the Lord went out from the threshold of the house (of Israel) . . . Ezk 10:18

Israel is compared to a useless fruit vine and a faithless bride. 'I pledged my self to you and entered into a covenant with you, says the Lord God, and you became mine.' Ezk 16:9

'But you trusted in your beauty, and played the whore because of your fame, and lavished whorings on any passer-by.' After all your wickedness (woe, woe to you! Says the Lord God) . . . . How sick is your heart . . . Ezk 16:23, 30

Jerusalem falls, but not forever.

Thus says the Lord God: Is it not for your sake, O house of Israel, that I am about to act, but for the sake of my holy name . . . I will sanctify my great name . . . . I will display my holiness before their eyes . . . . I will sprinkle clean water upon you, and you shall be clean from all your uncleanness . . . A new heart I will give you, and a new spirit I will put within you; and I will remove from your body the heart of stone and give you a heart of flesh. I will put my spirit within you, and make you follow my statues and be careful to observe my ordinances. Then you shall live . . . and you shall be my people, and I will be your God.' Ezk 36:22-28

Ezekiel ends with a vision of a new temple and return of the glory of God to the temple.

And the city shall be named 'The Lord is There.' Ezk 48:35

O Lord, remove my heart of stone and give me a new spirit. Amen.

34th Sunday – Read Daniel

'The God in whose power is your very breath, and to whom belong all your ways, you have not honored.' Dan 5:23

November 28, 2010

Daniel – is the only truly apocalyptic literature in the Hebrew Bible. The book is made of two sections. Chapters 1-6 are stories about Daniel and his friends who were portrayed as Jews in exile under King Nebuchadnezzar of Babylon. Chapters 7-12 are apocalyptic visions reported by Daniel judging and predicting the demise of the great world powers of the time.

Of course Christians and Jews interpret the book differently. Jews tend to think of Daniel as a book about a righteous man of God who displayed total loyalty and trust in God during exilic conditions (like Esther). Christians see the book as 'prefigurations of Christ and Christian resurrection' according to Lawrence Wills.

One interesting thing about the book is that some of it is written in Hebrew and some of it in Aramaic.

In the opening story King Nebuchadnezzar is looking for bench strength in his court. He calls 'Israelites of the royal family and of nobility, young men without physical defect and handsome, versed in every branch of wisdom, endowed with knowledge and insight, and competent to serve in the king's palace; they were to be taught the literature and language of the Chaldeans.' Dan 1:3-4

Daniel and his three friends were selected. They refused the royal rations so they could keep themselves pure subsisting on vegetables and water. The Bible reports Daniel had 'insight into all visions and dreams.' Dan 1:17

Nebuchadnezzar had an awful dream. None of his courtiers could interpret the dream. The king was going to have all the wise men killed. Daniel heard about the dilemma and prayed for God's mercy to grant him the wisdom to save the wise men. In a night vision, God granted Daniel his request and Daniel blessed the God of heaven:

'Blessed be the name of God from age to age, for wisdom and power are his . . . . He reveals deep and hidden things; he knows what is in the darkness, and light dwells within him.'

To you, O God of my ancestors, I give thanks and praise, for you have given me wisdom and power and have now revealed to me what we asked of you.' Dan 2:20-23

Daniel gave all the credit to God and interpreted the dream. Daniel told the king that God gave him immense earthly power and that Nebuchadnezzar squandered that gift. So, the king would be turned into a wild beast until he learned a little humility.

Nebuchadnezzar worshiped Daniel for the correct interpretation. Daniel and his friends were promoted in the royal court and this ticked off the old timers. They plotted against the new arrivals. A law was passed saying that everyone had to worship the king and a giant golden statue or be burned to death.

The Jewish boys stood firm, 'If our God whom we serve is able to deliver us from the furnace of blazing fire and out of your hand, O king, let him deliver us. But if not, be it known to you we will not serve your gods and we will not worship the golden statue that you have set up.' Dan 3:17

Nebuchadnezzar was so mad that the Jews won't worship him that 'He ordered the furnace heated up seven times more than was customary' Dan 3:19

Daniel's friends were saved in the fire by an angel and the king proclaimed the virtues and God again and granted the guys new promotions.

The king dreamed again and Daniel interpreted again in chapter 4. But this time the judgment was inflicted. 'Immediately the sentence was fulfilled against Nebuchadnezzar. He was driven away from human society, ate grass like an oxen, and his body was bathed with the dew of heaven, until his hair grew as long as eagles' feathers and his nails became like bird's claws. Dan 4:33

In the next chapter we learn about a new king, Nebuchadnezzar's son Belshazzar. The apple doesn't fall very far from the tree. Belshazzar held a great feast and used all the holy vessels captured from the Jewish temple as wine goblets. Mysterious writing appears on the wall during the feast. No one can interpret the writing so of course they call for Daniel. Daniel is offered a lot of loot to tell them what it means.

'Let your gifts be for yourself, or give them to someone else. Nevertheless, I will read the writing to the king and let him know the interpretation. Dan 5:17

Daniel told the young king about his father. How he was given kingship, greatness, glory and majesty . . . 'but his heart was lifted up and his spirit was hardened so that he acted proudly, he was deposed from his kingly throne and his glory was stripped of him.

. . . And you, Belshazzar his son have not humbled your heart, even though you knew all this! You have exalted yourself against the Lord of heaven! . . . you have praised all the false gods . . . but the God in whose power is your very breath, and to whom belong all your ways, you have not honored.' Dan 5:20-23

This time justice was not delayed, 'That very night Belshazzar, the Chaldean king was killed.' Dan 5:30

Perhaps the most famous story is about Daniel being thrown into the lions den by the next king whose name was Darius. Darius signed a decree stating that anyone who prayed to anyone except the king was to be thrown to the lions. Daniel got 'down on his knees thee times a day to pray to his God and praise him' . . . The conspirators came and found Daniel praying and seeking mercy before his God.' They tossed Daniel into the pit. But 'no kind of harm was found on him, because he had trusted in his God.' . . . So Daniel prospered during the reign of Darius and the reign of Cyrus the Persian. Dan 6:10-28

The final chapters are visions that Daniel had about all the persecuting powers of his time. Some people who read apocalyptic books interpret them as predicting the end times. Others see them as hopeful literature that served to hold a people together during exile and persecution.

I believe that some great faithful men of our past were able to see and know things beyond this world. But it should be noted that what these men saw in their visions was really beyond description. Ezekiel for example, who saw the glory of God, constantly used 'something like' in his writing. It is also worth pointing out that the Bible is clear humans are not to know such things as end times. No end-timer has been right yet. So we wait for the judgment of God and hope for His mercy.

35th Sunday – Read Hosea

'It's time to seek the Lord that He may come and rain righteousness upon you.' Hos 10:12

December 5, 2010

Hosea – a really old prophet. He wrote to the kings of the Northern Kingdom of Israel around 800 BCE. Hosea was a political critic. During his times, Israel felt pressure from the neighboring powers of Aram and Assyria to enter in alliances for its protection. The Northern Kingdom first sided with Assyria, and then later switched its loyalty to Aram when King Jeroboam's son Zechariah died. In 722 BCE, Assyria destroyed the

Northern Kingdom for good. But they were not destroyed without first hearing a blast from God.

Hosea heard the word of the Lord. According to Marvin Sweeny, Hosea was heavily involved in the debate concerning Israel's future and he severely criticized the alliances with foreign powers. Hosea saw the alliances as a rejection of trust in the Lord.

In the beginning of the book, God instructs Hosea to marry a hooker. He took Gomer as his wife and they had three children. Two of the children had interesting names: 'No mercy and 'they are not my people and I am not your God.' Hos 1:8 The story is replete with symbolism. Hosea's real life mirrors Israel's national and moral life. Hosea portrays Israel as an adulteress seeking safety and security first from one lover then another.

'The Lord said to me again, Go, love a woman who has a lover and is an adulteress, just as the Lord loves the people of Israel, though they turn to other gods and love raisin cakes.' Hos 3:1

'Hear the word of the Lord, O people of Israel, for the Lord has an indictment against the inhabitants of the land. There is no faithfulness or loyalty, and no knowledge of God in the land. Swearing, lying and murder and stealing and adultery break out; bloodshed follows bloodshed. Hos 4:1-2

'My people consult a piece of wood and divining rod gives them oracles . . . when their drinking is ended, they indulge in sexual orgies; they love lewdness more than their glory. Hos 4:7, 18-19

It is clear that even though we read images of an adulteress, it is the men who are the problem with Israel. The kings and priests are leading the people astray. 'Hear this, O priests . . . Listen O, kings for judgment pertains to you.' Hos 5:1-2

Hosea stresses a right relationship with God. 'For I desire a steadfast love and not sacrifice; the knowledge of God rather than burnt offerings. Hos 6:6

But no one will listen. 'The prophet is a fool, the man of spirit is mad.' Hos 9:7 'Because they have not listened to him, my God will reject them; they shall become wanders among the nations.' Hos 9:17

Hosea shouts the way to the people, kings and priests.

'For it is time to seek the Lord that he may come and rain righteousness upon you. Hos 10:12

Come back the prophet pleads. 'Return, O Israel, to the Lord your God, for you have stumbled because of your iniquity. Take words with you and return to the Lord. Those who are wise understand these things; those who are discerning know them. For the ways of the Lord are right, and the upright walk in them.' Hos 14:1-2, 9-10

Throughout the Old Testament we are told to be righteous (tsedekah). In 'The Prophets', Heschel writes, 'Righteous is not just a value; it is God's part of human life, God's stake in human history. The universe is done. The masterpiece still undone, in the process of being created, is history. For accomplishing His grand design, God needs the help of men . . . Life is clay, and righteousness is the mold in which God wants history to be shaped.'

Righteousness is much, much more than being good. How shall we go forth?

36th Sunday – Read Joel, Amos, Obadiah

'Take away from me the noise of your songs!.

But let justice roll down like waters, and righteousness like an ever-flowing stream.' Amos 5:23-24

December 12, 2010

Joel, Amos and Obadiah – are called Minor Prophets because their books are short not because their message is unimportant. Joel seems to have been written in about the 5th century BCE. We can associate the images used in the books to thefall of the Northern and Southern Kingdoms of Israel which were times of utter desolation and despair. According to Ehud Ben Zvi, Joel asks his hearers (not many could read back then) to 'imagine a terrifying plague of locusts and its horrifying impact on society and the natural environment created by human society. Then the locusts became a mighty army sent by the Lord against Judah.' The equivalent of nuclear holocaust happened. They were told though that it wasn't too late to return to God.

'Listen to this, O elders,
Give ear all inhabitants of the land,
Tell your children about it, and their children tell theirs,
And their children the next generation!
What the cutter has left, the locust has destroyed!
What the locust has left, the grub has devoured;
And what the grub has left, the hopper has devoured.

Wake up, you drunkards and weep!' Joel 1:1-5

Joel notes the only thing left to do.

'Solemnize a fast,
And cry out to the Lord. Joel 1:14

For great is the day of the Lord,
Most terrible-who can endure it?
'Yet even now'-says the Lord-
Turn back to Me with all your hearts,
And with fasting, weeping, and lamenting,

Rend your hearts
Rather than your garments,
And turn back to the Lord your God.
For He is gracious and compassionate,
Slow to anger, abounding in kindness.' Joel 2:11-14

Joel reminded the people that a day of renewal would come.

'I will repay you for the years consumed by swarms and hoppers.
My people shall be shamed no more.
After that I will pour out my spirit on all flesh

Your sons and daughters shall prophesy;
Your old men shall dream dreams
And your young men shall see visions' Joel 2:25, 3:1:2

Whereas Hosea was a political critic, Amos was a social critic who told the people why their nation had fallen. But he also follows the pattern of the prophets by providing for a hopeful time of restoration. So why did Israel fall?

'Because they have rejected the law of the Lord and have not kept his statues, but they have been led astray by the same lies after which their ancestors walked.' Amos 2:4

'Because they sell the righteous for silver,
And the needy for a pair of sandals
They who trample the head of the poor into the dust of the earth,
And push the afflicted out of the way.' Amos 2:6-7

'Hear this you cows of Bashan . . . who oppress the poor, crush the needy, who say to their husbands, 'Bring something to drink!'

I overthrew some of you, as when God overthrew Sodom and Gomorrah and you were like a brand snatched from the fire, yet you did not return to me . . . prepare to meet your God!' Amos 4:1-9

'Seek good and not evil that you may live.' Amos 5:14

'I hate, I despise your festivals, and I take no delight in your solemn assemblies . . .
Take away from me the noise of your songs,

But let justice roll down like waters,
And righteousness like an ever-flowing stream.' Amos 5:21-24

Amos closes with a description of a hopeful future.

'O Lord God, forgive, I beg you!
How can Jacob stand?
He is so small!
The Lord relented concerning this;
It shall not be, said the Lord.' Amos 7:1-3

'On that day I will raise up the booth of David that is fallen,
And repair its breaches,
And raise up its ruins,
And rebuild it as in the days of old.' Amos 9:11

Obadiah is the shortest book in the Hebrew Scriptures containing less than 300 Hebrew words. The primary message is one of judgment.

'Your arrogant heart has seduced you,
You who dwell in the clefts of the rock,
You think in your heart,
Who can pull me down to earth?
Should you nest as high as an eagle,
Should your eyrie be lodged among the stars,
Even from there I will pull you down-declares the Lord. Obad 1:3-4

As you did, so shall it be done to you;
Your conduct shall be requited.
Yea, against all nations
The day of the Lord is at hand Obad 1:15

But on Zion's mount a remnant shall survive,
And it shall be holy Obad 1:17

The prophet Joel did not call attention to himself. Amos was a sheepherder and a dresser of sycamore trees. Who knows about Obadiah? But the message of the prophet is clear: seek justice and righteousness and be holy because the Lord God is Holy. But the Bible is also clear on this; we can't do it.

It has been a beautiful Christmas season for me this year. One of the most breathtaking moments came Christmas Eve morning. As I exited the highway heading to work, a very reverent version of Silent Night began playing on the radio. I was in such a good mood, for the special time with family was only hours away. As I rolled to a stop the car next to me was thumping. Bass and dirty lyrics were washing out the sound of my moving music. How depressing I thought it was that the person next to me didn't seem to have any thoughts about God on the eve of Christmas. And I knew that this was exactly the state of mind to which the prophet was speaking.

Our predicament is sad in a way. Either we don't think about God at all and live with a God shaped hole in us, or we 'make it' and end up believing how clever we are. There's something larger going on. Fasting, lamenting, and crying out to the Lord is needed by all.

O you cows of Bashan! Bring me something to drink!

37th Sunday – Read Jonah, Micah, Nahum

'What does He require of you but to do justice, and to love kindness, and to walk humbly with your God.' Micah 6:8

December 19, 2011

Jonah, Micah, Nahum – Jonah seems like a story about how not to be a prophet. Jonah gets called by God to witness to the non-Jewish community of Nineveh (arch enemy). He doesn't want to do this so he gets on a ship to run away and the deckhands think he is the cause of a major storm tossing their ship to and fro. The shipmates throw Jonah into the sea and he swallowed by a large fish. Jonah, as we often do, gets real religion when he is in trouble.

'I called to the Lord out of my distress and he answered me . . . . As my life was ebbing away, I remembered the Lord.' Jonah 2:1, 7

'Then the Lord spoke to the fish and it spewed Jonah out upon the dry land.' Jonah 2:10

'Then the word of the Lord came to Jonah a second time, saying 'Get up, go to Nineveh that great city and proclaim the message that I tell you.' Jonah 3:1

This time Jonah went.

Ehud Ben VI said that strangely enough Jonah was the most successful of all the prophets. He spoke one sentence to the people of Nineveh and they repented from their evil ways and turned to praising God. God saw this and spared the city from destruction.

'But this was very displeasing to Jonah, and he became angry! 4:1 Jonah prayed to God saying he would rather die than have these people saved. Jonah was sitting in the hot sun and God grew a bush to provide him shade. The next day the bush withered up and Jonah was angry with God again.

God rebukes Jonah "You are concerned about the bush, for which you did not labor and which you did not grow . . . And should I not be concerned about Nineveh, that great city, in which there are more than 120,000 persons who do not know their right hand from their left hand? Jonah 4:10-11

There are lots of points to be raised from the reading of this short book. For me, it is insightful into our own human nature. Why is it that we are resentful of good things when they happen to people who are not like us? Why is it that we only really pray when we get in trouble? Why is it that we pout and whine we things don't go our way? Why is it that we don't answer God's call the first time? Why do we have to be taught so many lessons? Why is it that we don't trust in the providence of God?

On to Micah! Micah was a prophet who saw the end of the Northern Kingdom and the first years of Judah's existence as the sole remaining tribe. Judith Sanderson reminds us that Micah preached 'that David's city will, indeed, fall to the enemy, precisely because Judah in not obeying the terms of the covenant with Israel delivered through Moses. That covenant was established after the liberation of Israel from slavery and it requires Israel to maintain justice precisely because it experienced such terrible injustice in Egypt.'

This is interesting after we have just read where Jonah did not want the foreigners to be spared the Lord's judgment.

In true prophetic style Micah calls out Judah for its behavior, lets them know why they are being punished and provided a glimpse of a more hopeful future.

'Hear, you peoples, all of you . . . . For lo, the Lord is coming out of his place and will come down and tread upon the high places of the earth.' Mic 1:2-3

'Alas for those who devise wickedness and when the morning dawns they perform it, because it is in their power. They cover fields, and seize them; house, and take them away; they oppress householder and house, people their inheritance.

Now, I am devising against this family and evil from which you cannot remove your necks; and you shall not walk haughtily.' Mic 2:1-3

'Hear this, you rulers of the house of Jacob and chiefs of the house of Israel who abhor justice and pervert all equity, who build Zion with blood and Jerusalem with wrong! Mic 3:9-10

But there is a time in the future to look forward to. 'But you, O Bethlehem, who are one of the little clans of Judah, from you shall come forth from me one who is to rule in Israel who origin is from old.

And he shall stand and feed his flock in the strength of the Lord in the majesty of the name of the Lord his God. And they shall live secure, for now he shall be great to the ends of the earth; and he shall be the one of peace.' Mic 5:2-5

People want to know what God wants them to do. Micah tells them what they already know: 'He has told you, O mortal, what is good; and what does he require of you but to do justice, and to love kindness, and to walk humbly with your God? Mic 6:8

Micah closes by telling everyone what he plans to do: 'But as for me, I will look to the Lord, I will wait for the God of my salvation and my God will hear me. Mic 7:7

In the span of a few short chapters, we have Jonah convincing a great city of an arch enemy to repent and turn to God. They do so and are spared. We have Micah castigating the Jewish people for treating foreigners poorly because they were once foreigners in a land themselves. But Nahum has no time for any of this. The power that had battered and badgered the region as superpower for over 200 years was finished. Nahum was clearly glad that Nineveh, the capital city of Assyria, was destroyed. Carol Stuhlmueller writes 'His theology is focused upon one consuming topic: God does not tolerate injustice forever!

And so we read: 'An oracle concerning Nineveh. A jealous and avenging God is the Lord, the Lord is avenging and wrathful; the Lord takes vengeance to his adversaries and rages against his enemies. The Lord is slow to anger but great in power, and the Lord will by no means clear the guilty.' Nah 1:1-2

As gleeful as Nahum was that Nineveh was destroyed, he is sure that trusting in the Lord is better than relying on oneself.

'The Lord is good, a stronghold in the day of trouble; he protects those who take refuge in him.' Nah 1:7

But the end has come upon Nineveh.

'A shatterer has come up against you. Guard your ramparts; watch the road; gird up your loins; collect all your strength . . . Devastation, desolation and destruction! Hearts faint and knees tremble, all loins quake, all faces grow pale. Nah 2:1, 10

Nineveh is devastated; who will bemoan her? Where shall I seek comforters for you?' All who hear this news of you clap their hands over you.' Nah 3:7, 19

Irene Nowell says that a subtle theme of Nahum may be that of a lesson for Judah. If Judah does not mend her ways then she might befall the same fate as the defeated city of Nineveh. She also writes "The message is also for today's world. If we trust in God, no enemy can destroy us; if we turn away from God and trust in ourselves, we are in mortal danger.'

38th Sunday – Read Habakkuk, Zephaniah

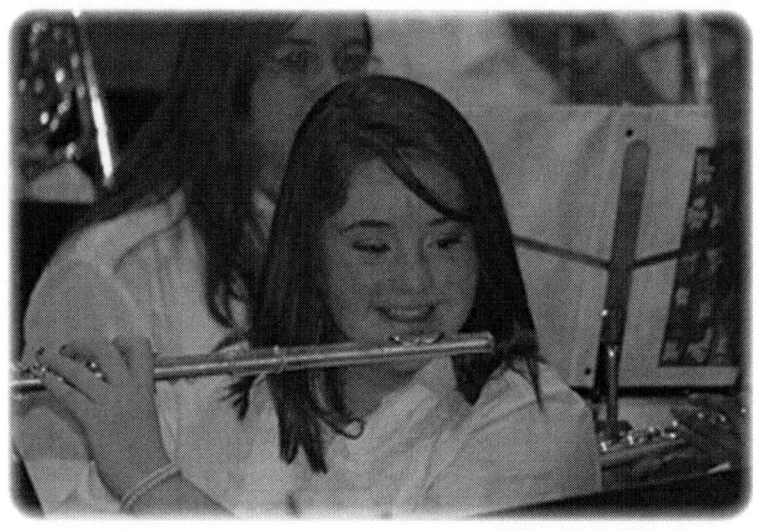

'Look at the proud! Their spirit is not right in them. But the righteous live by faith.' Hab 2:4

December 26, 2010

Habakkuk and Zephaniah – Habakkuk makes his point right off the bat. The terrible Babylonians were making life miserable for everybody else.

Their horses are swifter than leopards, more menacing than wolves at dusk; their horses charge . . . Then they sweep like the wind; they transgress and become guilty; their own might is their god! Hab 1:8,11'

'How long, O Lord, shall I cry out and you not listen . . . why do you make me see wrongdoing and look at trouble? The wicked surround the righteous-therefore justice comes forth perverted . . . . Look at the nations and see! Be astonished! Be astounded! For a work is being done in your days that you would not believe if you were told.' Hab 1:2-5

Habakkuk is not afraid to raise questions to God. The Bible writers let their angst rise up. This is a far cry from the polite and pleasure seeking worship that we perform today.

God responds to Habakkuk. 'Write the vision: make it plain on tablets, so that a runner may read it. For there is a vision for the appointed time; it speaks of the end and does not lie. If it seems to tarry, wait for it; it will surely come, it will not delay.

Look at the proud! Their spirit is not right in them. But the righteous live by faith.' 2:2-4

As followers of God, we are called to watch and wait. We are called to live by faith. The prophets were wisest and the most faithful of our oldest and yet they did not have an easy road to hoe. They had hard questions for God. The responses they got were not quick fixes. Be patient, wait, and stay strong.

'Though the fig tree does not blossom, and no fruit is on the vines; though the produce of the olive fails, and the fields yield no food . . . yet I will rejoice in the Lord; I will exult in the God of my salvation. God, the Lord is my strength.' Hab 3:17-18

Because one day 'earth will be filled with the knowledge of the glory of the Lord.' Hab 2:14

Zephaniah – appears to have lived in the period around Judah's last great King Josiah. But the book does not list the good deeds of the king. Instead Zephaniah pronounces judgment. Ehud Ben Zvi tells us that there is lots of wordplay in the book 'and potential or actual ambiguities that channel the attention of the readers and contribute to the possibility of multiple readings. These features are typical in prophetic books because they facilitate the continuous reading and study of these texts . . . . as do all prophetic books, Zephaniah includes prophecies of hope. Even the announcements of doom against Judah serve, in part, to emphasize hope from the perspective of the post monarchic readers.'

Right into the text then. 'I will sweep everything away from the face of the earth- declares the Lord . . . I will stretch out my arm against Judah and against all who dwell in Jerusalem; And I will wipe out from this place every vestige of Baal.' Zeph 1:2-4

'The great day of the Lord is near; near and hastening fast.' Zeph 1:14

Gather together, gather O shameless nation, before you are driven away like the drifting chaff . . . . seek the Lord, all you humble of the land, who do his commands; seek righteousness, seek humility; perhaps you make be hidden on the day of the Lord's wrath.' Zeph 2:1-3

'Therefore wait for me, says the Lord, for the day when I arise as a witness . . . At that time, I will change the speech of the peoples to a pure speech, that all of them may call on the name of the Lord and serve him with one accord . . . For I will leave in the midst of you a people of humble and lowly. They shall seek refuge in the name of the Lord . . . . I will save the lame and gather the outcast and I will change their shame into praise and renown in all the earth. At that time I will bring you home.' Zeph 3:8,9,12, 19, 20

39th Sunday – Read Haggai, Zechariah, Malachi

'See I am sending my messenger to prepare the way before me, and the Lord whom you seek will suddenly come to his temple.' Mal 3:1

January 2, 2011

Haggai, Zechariah, Malachi – As we complete our reading of the Hebrew Scriptures Ehud Ben Zvi writes 'In Jewish tradition, Haggai, Zechariah, and Malachi are the last prophets; after them prophecy ceases. According to tradition, they were among the members of the 'Great Assembly' a group that was the precursor of the Sanhedrin, and after their death, the Holy Spirit departed from Israel. Though, 'bat kol' (the daughter of the voice, or echo) remained available to Israel.'

Haggai is one of the few biblical books that are precisely dated. So it is clear that Haggai is writing about the rebuilding of the temple after it had been destroyed in 586BC.

With reproach and encouragement the prophet sets about to state what he heard from the Lord. 'Is it a time for you yourselves to live in your paneled house, while this house lies in ruins? Now, therefore thus says the Lord of hosts: Consider how you have fared. You have sown much but harvested little; you eat, but you have enough; you drink, but you never have your fill; you cloth yourselves, but no one is warm; and you that earn wages earn wages to put them in a bag with holes . . . Go up to the hills and bring wood and build the house, so that I may take pleasure in it and be honored.' Mal 1:3-7

For a change the people listen. 'The people obeyed the voice of the Lord their God and the words of the prophet Haggai . . . . The Haggai, the messenger of the Lord spoke to the people with the Lord's message saying "I am with you.' Mal 1:12-13

Remember 'The silver is mine, and the gold is mine, says the Lord of hosts. The latter splendor of this house shall be greater that the former . . . and in this place I will give prosperity.' Mal 2:8

Zechariah is also written around the same time as Haggai. The book is also concerned with the rebuilding of the temple. But Zechariah according the Ehud Ben Zvi 'emphasizes repentance and exhorts the community directly addressed within the book, and above all, that of the readership to behave in accordance with the divine will, so as to avoid the fate of their ancestors.'

'Turn back to me says the Lord of hosts- and I will turn back to you . . . do not be like your fathers.' Zech 1:3-4

Zechariah also has some really interesting visions and dialogue with angels of God who were sent to 'patrol the earth.' Zech 1:10

'Then the angel of the Lord assured Joshua, saying, If you will walk in my ways and keep my requirements, the you shall rule my house and have charge of my courts.' Zech 3:6

Evidently people forgot or did not hear the messages of the other prophets. It has to constantly be repeated. Maybe that is why we need to go to church once on Sunday and then again on Wednesday lest we forget too.

The word of the Lord came to Zechariah saying, render true judgments, show kindness and mercy to one another; do not oppress the widow, the orphan, the alien, or the poor; and do not devise evil in your hearts against one another.' Zech 7:8-10

If the people listen then 'They shall be my people and I will be their God, in faithfulness and in righteousness.' Zech 8:8

'These are the things that you shall do: Speak the truth to one another, render in your gates judgments that are true and make for peace. Do no devise evil in your hearts against one another and love no false oath, for all these things I hate, says the Lord.' Zech 8:16-17

There is also a lot of imagery of different kinds of shepherds in chapter 11. We have to have read the Hebrew Scriptures to fully appreciate the Good Shepherd we are going to read about next.

Malachi is the last book in the Hebrew Scriptures. The name means 'My Messenger.' Ben Zvi again, 'The readers of the book of Malachi are asked to look at some pitfalls in everyday life and in the cult at the Temple, and particularly at how they affect the relationship between the Lord and Israel, resulting in a lack of prosperity. Issues concerning proper offerings, marriage practices, and tithes are especially prominent in the book.'

Ben Zvi notes that through Malachi God promises to send his prophet Elijah back to earth and there will be 'a final liberation, one even greater that the exodus from Egypt, for after Israel's first liberation it eventually became enslaved, but it will not after the one promised in Malachi.'

Finally Malachi joins a list of prophets who have lots of questions for God such as 'Where is the God of justice?'

Malachi bemoans all the bickering going on in Israel. "Have we not all one father? Has not one God, created us? Whey then are we faithless to one another, profaning the covenant of our ancestors? Mal 2:10

You have wearied the Lord with your words. Yet you say, how have we wearied him? By saying, all who do evil are good in the sight of the Lord, and he delights in them. Or by asking, 'Where is the God of justice? Mal 2:17

'See I am sending my messenger to prepare the way before me, and the Lord whom you seek will suddenly come to his temple . . . . but who can endure the day of his coming, and who can stand when he appears.' Mal 3:1-2

'Then I will draw near to you for judgment: I will be swift to bear witness against the sorcerers, against the adulterers, against those who swear falsely, against those who oppress the hired workers in their wages, the widow and the orphan, against those who thrust aside the alien, and do not fear me, says the Lord . . . . For I the Lord do not change . . . Return to me and I will return to you.' Mal 3:5-7

'How shall we return? Will anyone rob God? Yet you are robbing me!. In your tithes and offerings! Bring me the full tithe into the storehouse, that that there may be food in my house, and thus put me to the test, says the Lord of hosts. See if I will not open the windows of heaven for you and pour down for you an overflowing blessing.' Mal 3:8-10

'See the day is coming, burning like and oven, when all the arrogant and all evildoers will be stubble . . . But for you who revere my name the sun of righteousness shall rise, with healing in its wings . . . . remember the teaching of my servant Moses, the statues and ordinances that I commanded him at Horeb for all Israel.'. Mal 4:1-5

40th Sunday – Read Matthew

'Blessed are the meek, for they will inherit the earth.'

January 9, 2011

The Gospel of Jesus Christ according to Matthew – The problem is we're stuck between two songs. Sometimes we feel like the Uncle Kracker song 'Good to be me"

'Damn, I got it all figured out
I got no worries that I'm worried about
It's like I caught some crazy, happy disease
Damn, it feels good to be me'

And then bam it's like the Sugarland song 'You might just make me believe'

'I got miles of trouble spreadin' far and wide
Bills on the table gettin' higher and higher
They just keep on comin', there ain't no end in sight
I'm just holdin' on tight'

When we feel like we have it all figured out we forget about God. When trouble starts spreading far and wide we cry out to God that life isn't fair.

Consider the biblical journey so far and it's not pretty. Eve ate the forbidden fruit, Adam blamed Eve, Eve blamed the snake, Cain killed his brother Able, Noah drank too much wine, Abraham and Sarah laughed at God, Rebecca and Jacob tricked Esau, Rachel stole some figurines, Moses killed an Egyptian, the Hebrew people whined because they didn't have gourmet food in the desert, Saul tried to kill David, David lusted after Bathsheba, David's son raped his sister, the other kings were more rotten than their fathers had been and on and on and on.

For this broken world, a Savior is needed.

Matthew then probably wrote his gospel 50 years after the death of Christ. It is believed that Matthew used the book of Mark and other sources known as Q as reference material. He wrote to a local Jewish audience struggling to maintain its Jewish traditions on the one hand and on the other trying to develop itself into a new Christian community.

Thomas Long in his Westminster Bible Companion Commentary writes that 'Matthew's setting was one where a people had to carve out an identity among many competing possibilities, and much of the Gospel is aimed at helping Matthew's church define its distinct Christian character in a confusing world of rival claims. '

The rival Jewish claim was that a Messiah would come to set things right. An exiled community that trusted in God thought it would be a mighty king in the fashion of David who was a great warrior. This warrior king would defeat all the mighty powers and Israel would live forever in peace and harmony.

Matthew begins his Gospel by linking Jesus all the way back to Abraham. "An account of the genealogy of Jesus the Messiah, the son of David, the son of Abraham.' Matt 1:1

Long: "Matthew opens his Gospel with a genealogy and, by doing so, discloses the true identity of Jesus . . . Jesus is the culmination of all of Israel's history, the goal of their messianic hopes, the embodiment of their hunger for a true and perfect king, and the fulfillment of the promise to become a blessing to the whole human race.'

A significant fact is that five women are listed in the family tree. Each of these women according to Long has 'questionable character' or come from non-Israelite stock. But through these women history is changed.' God is surprising and history is shaped in ways we might not imagine.

Matthew reports that Jesus is conceived through the Holy Spirit by unwed peasant girl named Mary.

'Look the virgin shall conceive and bear a son and they shall name his Emmanuel.' Isaiah 7:14

Matthew indeed knew his Hebrew Scripture. Long: 'this strategy of quoting Old Testament prophecy and announcing its fulfillment in the life of Jesus is a favorite of Matthew's. Nearly a dozen times Matthew explicitly connects something with Jesus to a passage from one of the prophets.'

When the time in history was right, John the Baptist stood in the desert shouting:

'Repent, for the kingdom of heaven has come near. The voice of one crying out in the wilderness: Prepare the way of the Lord, make his paths straight.' Matt 3:2-3

The kingdom is heaven is basically the idea that everything opposed to God and His ways will be destroyed. In coming near Matthew proclaims that Jesus 'embodied and expressed the peace, love and mercy that God wills for all people,' according to Long.

I think we moderns are turned off by the phrase repent perhaps because of the guy with the rainbow hair at the football game holding up the poster.

Or the furniture truck we see from a small town with King James verses printed on the side 'Repent ye or perish in a lake of fire.'

But for Long, "Repentance does not mean feeling sorry about the things one has done wrong or guilty about one's past. Repentance is a basic reorientation of one's life. In repentance one turns from one framework of meaning to another, from one way of thinking about self, others, God and life to another competing and compelling vision . . . . This means coming to the recognition that one has been basing one's life on a lie, on a flawed view of what is true and of lasting value.'

Before his ministry began, Jesus was tempted by Satan. But because he knew his Hebrew Scriptures Jesus thwarted the devil's plans.

'One does not live by bread alone but by every word that comes from the mouth of God.' Matt 4:4 (Deut 8:3)

Jesus began his ministry by uttering the same words used by John the Baptist. 'Repent, for the kingdom of heaven has come near.' 4:12 He then calls his first two disciples Simon Peter and Andrew. 'Follow me, and I will make you fish for people. Immediately they left their nets and followed him.' 4:18-19

From the immediate response of the first disciples, the theological message is clear. The nature of the Gospel is the upside down. Long: 'the kingdom of heaven does not exist to serve families, but families exist to serve the kingdom of heaven.'

What is so upside down about Jesus' message? Consider the Sermon on the Mount:

'Then he began to speak, and taught them, saying:

Blessed are the poor in spirit, for theirs is the kingdom of heaven.
Blessed are those who mourn, for they will be comforted.
Blessed are the meek, for they will inherit the earth.
Blessed are those who hunger and thirst for righteousness, for they will be filled.
Blessed are the merciful, for they will receive mercy.
Blessed are the pure in heart, for they will see God.

Blessed are the peacemakers, for they will be called children of God. Blessed are those who are persecuted for righteousness' sake, for theirs is the kingdom of heaven.' Matt 5:2-11

Long: 'The Beatitudes declare that the poor in spirit, the meek, the peacemakers are the ones who are truly blessed. We live in a world; however, that pronounces the benediction over the self-sufficient, the assertive, and the power brokers. The people who the world would see as pitiful – the mournful, the persecuted-are the people Jesus claims are truly joyful.'

So we are called to be humble to 'let your light shine before others, so that they may see your good works and give glory to your Father in heaven.' Matt 5:16

Was Jesus' message counter cultural? Oh yes. 'You have heard it said, you shall not commit adultery. But I say to you that everyone who looks at a woman with lust has already committed adultery with her in his heart . . . . Do not resist an evildoer. Love your enemies and pray for those who persecute you . . . Be perfect, therefore, as your heavenly Father is perfect. Matt 5:21-48

There is more . . . Give your gifts in secret and do not sound a trumpet before you . . . . go in to your closet and pray . . . . when you fast, put oil on your head and wash your face so no one can tell. Matt 6:1-8

'Do not store up treasures for yourself on earth, for where your treasure is, there your heart will be also . . . . Do not worry about what we will eat, drink or wear . . . but strive first for the kingdom of God and his righteousness, and all these things will be given to you as well.' 6:19-34

'Do not judge, so that you may not be judged.' 7:1 Long: Jesus requires that before we call for transformation of someone else, we be transformed ourselves.

Whoever becomes humble like this child is the greatest in the kingdom of heaven.

Jesus then performs his first healings: Long: 'Each of the persons healed -a leper and Gentile, and a woman-is on the edges of Israelite society.'

Jesus also sat down to eat with the lowly of society. The Pharisees ask 'why does your teacher eat with tax collectors. Jesus replied 'Those who are well have no need of a physician, but those who are sick. Go and learn what this means. I desire mercy, not sacrifice. For I have come to call not the righteous but sinners. 9:9-17

Jesus sets the stage for his disciples in the future. 'When he saw the crowds, he had compassion for them, because they were harassed and helpless, like sheep without a shepherd. Then he said to his disciples, the harvest in plentiful, but the laborers are few, therefore ask the Lord of the harvest to send out laborers into his harvest.' 9:35-38

Jesus continues his ministry as Long notes teaching, preaching and healing. In all of this Jesus is showing us the kingdom of heaven. The kingdom is hidden to those that live for themselves. The kingdom is far from all things that oppose the will of god.

And the people in positions of power were offended by Jesus' message.

He came to his hometown and began to teach the people in their synagogue, so that they were astounded and said, where did this man get this wisdom and these deeds of power" Is not this a carpenter's son? Is not his mother called Mary . . . And they took offense at him.' Matt 13:54-58

'Do you know the Pharisees took offense when they heard what you said?' Matt 15:12

Long writes that the offenses is 'the clash between ceremonial religious ritual and the deeper will of God . . . . The religious leaders have suggested that Jesus' disciples do not love the will of God because they do not honor tradition. Jesus reverses this and accuses the leaders of loving the tradition instead of the will of God.'

From that time on, Jesus began to show his disciples that he must go to Jerusalem and undergo great suffering at the hand of the elders and chief priests and scribes, and be killed, and on the third day be raised.' Matt 16:21

But the people did not see, the leaders were offended, the disciples did not fully trust.

The song 'Sweet Little Jesus Boy' has it about right:
'Long time ago You were born
Born in a manger
Sweet little Jesus boy
The world treats You mean Lord,
Treats me mean too
But that's how things are down here
We didn't know who you were'

Who could believe that the Messiah would be crucified? Long writes 'The Messiah is supposed to save and liberate God's people, not be killed by oppressors. The idea of a crucified Messiah violates religious expectation and defies reason.'

And so we are told, 'if any want to become my followers, let them deny themselves and take up their cross and follow me.' Matt 16:24

Long: Taking up the cross 'means following in the way of Jesus, and that involves standing with those who are weak, opening doors to those who are unacceptable, loving those who are unlovely. Cross bearers forfeit the game of power before the first inning; they are never selected as 'Most Likely to Succeed' . . .

'It is the mystery of the gospel that what appears to crush everything one hopes to be as a human being-bearing the cross of service and suffering-is in fact the only way for a human being to be fully alive.'

Who is the greatest in the kingdom of heaven? . . . Truly I tell you, unless you change and become like little children, you will never enter the kingdom of heaven. Whoever becomes humble like this child is the greatest in the kingdom of heaven.' Whoever welcomes one such child in my name welcomes me.' Matt 18:1-5

Long: 'A low, humble, and insignificant child is the model for greatness in the kingdom. Jesus is teaching his disciples that leaders in the community of faith must be humble and unassuming. Faithful leadership is not a matter of winning at church politics or acquiring the trappings of prestige. It is being childlike and humble. The 'great ones' in the community of faith are not to be found tipping the maitre d' at a power lunch but serving the Lord's Supper in a cancer ward.'

Good at keeping the law, 'The young man said, I have kept all these, what do I lack? Jesus said to him, if you wish to be perfect, go, sell your possession, and give the money to the poor, and you will have treasure in heaven; then come and follow me . . . . Again I tell you, it is easier for a camel to go through the eye of a needle that for someone who is rich to enter the Kingdom of God . . . Then who can be saved? For mortals it is impossible, but for God all things are possible. Matt 19:20-26

Long: 'Alas the young man is too heavily invested in the status quo, in the world as it is; he cannot bear to part with his land and goods, so he turns away, grieving. He is offered the adventure of being a disciple of Jesus, a child of God with great treasure in heaven; he decides instead to manage real estate in Palestine.'

'Whoever wishes to be first among you must be your servant, just as the Son of Man came not be served but to serve, and give his life a ransom for many.' Matt 20:27-28

Jesus arrives in Jerusalem 'humble and mounted on a donkey.' Matt 21:5 He clears the temple "My house shall be called a house of prayer; but you make it a den of robbers.' Matt 21:13

The chief priests and scribes became angry. The Sadducees and Pharisees kept trying to trick Jesus. 'Which commandment is the law is the greatest? He said to them you shall love the Lord your god with all your heart, and with all your soul, and with all your mind. This is the greatest and first commandment. And a second is like it: You shall love your neighbor as yourself. On these two commandments hang all the law and the prophets.' Matt 22:36-40

Long: 'The whole law, said Jesus, every one of those 613 commandments, is really about love-loving God and loving neighbor.'

Long: 'Now, the Gospel of Matthew, which began with the roll call of birth, moves to a close with the account of the Messiah's death.'

'Then Jesus went with them to a place called Gethsemane; and he said to his disciples, 'Sit here while I go over there and pray . . . And going a little farther, he threw himself on the ground and prayed, my Father, if it is possible, let this cup pass from me; yet not what I want but what you want.' Matt 21:38-41

When Jesus came back he found the disciples asleep. 'The spirit is indeed willing, but the flesh is weak . . . . Get up, let us be going. See, my betrayer is at hand.' Matt 26:45-46

Jesus was betrayed by Judas into the hands of the chief priests and the elders of the people.

'Then the high priest said to him, 'I put you under oath before the living God, tell us if you are the Messiah, the Son of God. Jesus said to him, You have said so. But I tell you,

From now on you will see the Son of Man
Seated at the right hand of Power
And coming on the clouds of heaven.

Then the high priest tore his clothes and said 'He has blashphemed! Why do we still need witnesses? . . . What is your verdict? They answered 'He deserves death. Then they spat in his face and struck him; and some slapped him, saying, Prophecy to us, you Messiah! Who is it that struck you!'

Peter runs away and denies three times that he knows Jesus. Judas hangs himself. Pontius Pilate washed his hands of the situation and let the people crucify the living God.

'The soldier's . . . stripped him and put a scarlet robe on him, and after twisting some thorns into a crown, they put it on his head. The put a reed in his right hand and knelt before him, and too the reed and struck him on the head. After mocking him, they stripped him of the robe and put his own clothes on him. Then they led him away to crucify him.'

'You who would destroy the temple and build it again in three days, save yourself

'About three o'clock in the afternoon Jesus cried with a loud voice Eli, Eli, lema sabbachthani,? That is, My God, My God, why have you forsaken me?'

Jesus died on the cross and was placed in a tomb. The only ones who did not desert Jesus were the women. 'Many women were also there, looking on from a distance; they had followed Jesus from Galilee and had provided for him.' Matt 26, 27

The women came back to the tomb and an angel appeared to them. 'Do not be afraid, I know that you are looking for Jesus who was crucified. He is not here for he has been raised.'

The women go and tell the other disciples what has happened. The first preachers of the good news were women!

Jesus appears to the disciples and said to them 'All authority in heaven and on earth has been given to me. Go therefore and make disciples of all nations, baptizing them in the name of the Father and of the Son and of the Holy Spirit and teaching them to obey everything that I have commanded you. And remember, I am with you always, to the end of the age.' Matt 28

Long: 'This parting, but enduring, word from the risen Christ is the heart of Matthew's whole Gospel. As the church goes out with fear and joy, faith and doubt, devotion and dread to do the work of Christ, it is not promised success at every turn, a glad welcome in every heart, or even freedom from persecution and suffering. What the church is promised is that God in Christ will not abandon us but is present in the midst of the faithful-loving, encouraging, guiding, and giving hope.' Amen

41st Sunday – Read Mark

'I believe; help my unbelief!' Mark 9:24

January 16, 2011

The Good News about Jesus Christ according to Mark – That there are four Gospels about Jesus Christ which do not exactly match in every detail give some reason to dismiss their authenticity. Does anyone doubt that what the 'Father of History' Herodotus wrote was true? Historians have eight copies of his writing that date to 1300 years after his death. We are taught by historians to believe that words written by Herodotus are facts. The Gospels do not get the same such treatment. Perhaps it's an agenda thing. G.K. Chesterton said 'It's not that Christianity has been tried and found difficult, it's that Christianity has been found difficult and left untried.'

In his book, 'Alpha Questions of Life', Nicky Gumbel writes, 'The history of Thucydides is known almost entirely from eight manuscripts from about A.D. 900. The same is true of the history of Herodotus. Yet no classical scholar doubts the authentic of these works, in spite of the large time gap (events and age of manuscript copies) and the relatively few manuscripts. In regards to the New Testament, we have a great wealth of material. The New Testament was probably written between A.D 40 and 100. We have excellent full manuscripts of the whole New Testament dating from as early as A.D 350 (a time span of only three hundred years), papyri containing most of the New Testament writings dating from the third century, and even a fragment of John's Gospel dating from about A.D 130. There are over five thousand Greek manuscripts, over then thousand Latin manuscripts, and 9,300 other manuscripts, as well as over then thirty six thousand citing in the writings of the early church fathers. As one of the greatest textual critics ever, F.J.A. Hort, said, 'In the variety and fullness of the evidence on which it rests the text of the New Testament stand absolutely and unapproachably alone among ancient prose writings.'

I think another reason we can trust the Gospels is because they don't try and prop up the main characters. In most classical stories the main guys are portrayed as unbeatable. Mark Roberts wrote a book called 'Can we Trust the Gospels.' He writes, 'Given the centrality of the apostles, especially the first disciples, in the church's claim to rightful authority, it is fascinating and telling to note how the disciples are portrayed in the New Testament Gospels. They are after all the first leaders of the church. They are the ones from whom the church drew its power. Yet they are the ones whom the Gospel portrays as . . . . well . . . faithless, foolish, and unreliable.

Roberts cites the following as evidence:

-'The disciples consistently misunderstand Jesus':

'People were bringing little children to him in order that he might touch them; and the disciples spoke sternly to them. But when Jesus saw this, he was indignant and said to them, 'Let the little children come to me; do not stop them; for it is to such as these that the kingdom of God belongs. Mark 10:13-14

-'They are self-seeking, concerned for their own greatness':

'But they were silent, for on the way they had argued with one another about who was the greatest.' Mark 9:34

-'They lack faith in God or Jesus':

'He said to them, 'Why are you afraid? Have you still no faith?' Mark 4:40

-'They abandon Jesus in his hour of greatest need, sleeping while he asks them to join him in prayer at Gethsemane.'

'Sit here while I pray.' . . . He came and found them sleeping; and he said to Peter, 'Simon, are you asleep? Could you not keep awake one hour? Mark 14:32-43

'Then, when he is arrested, all of them desert Jesus and run away to save their own necks':

'All of them deserted him and fled.' Mark 14-50

'After the resurrection, the disciples disbelieve Mary's report that Jesus is risen.'

'But these words seemed to them an idle tale, and they did not believe them.' Luke 24:11

Roberts: 'The portrayal of the disciples in the Gospels strongly suggests that the early Christian tradition and the four evangelists were willing to pass on the truth even if that truth portrayed their founding leaders in an embarrassing light.'

'Christians in the first and second centuries believed some astounding things about Jesus. They believed that he was, not only the ultimate purveyor of God's wisdom but divine Wisdom in the flesh. They affirmed that Jesus was the Messiah of Israel; the one who had begun to inaugurate the kingdom of God on earth . . . The first Christians didn't just believe these things. They went around trying to get everybody else to believe them too.'

Mark then wanted people to believe what he believed. He was probably a follower of Peter. When Peter came under persecution in Rome, Mark wanted to get the story down on paper. Mark is breathless in his writing of the Gospel. Quick and hurried is his pace.

Whereas Matthew takes his time laying out the case for Christ in 28 chapters, Mark makes his point in a mere 16 chapters. He does not take the time to list a family history or any information surrounding the birth of Jesus. Mark starts with the ministry of Jesus.

'The beginning of the Good News of Jesus Christ, the Son of God.' 1:1

The catholic encyclopedia reports that in Mark's Gospel, 'Special attention is paid throughout to the human feelings and emotions of Christ, and to the effect produced by His miracles upon the crowd.'

'Filled with compassion, Jesus reached out his hand and touched the man. Mark 1:41

Jesus tried to get away from the crowds, 'Yet the people still came to him from everywhere. Mark 1:45

'This amazed everyone and they praised God saying, we have never seen anything like this.' Mark 2:12

'He looked around at them at them in anger and deeply distressed at their stubborn hearts.' Mark 3:5

'When Jesus landed and saw a large crowd, he had compassion on them, because they were like sheep without a shepherd. So he began teaching them many things.' Mark 6:34

'My soul is overwhelmed with sorrow to the point of death, he said to them.' Mark 14:34

There are several items in the Gospel of Mark that are unique among the Gospels, two of which are interesting to me. First is this report:

'A certain young man was following him, wearing nothing but a linen cloth. They caught hold of him, but he left the linen cloth and ran off naked.' Mark 14:51-52. Could this have been a young Mark who later followed the Apostle Peter to Rome?

Also, unique among the Gospels is the commissioning of the disciples:

'Later he appeared to the eleven themselves as they were sitting at the table; and he upbraided them for their lack of faith and stubbornness, because they had not believed those who saw him after he had risen. And he said to them, 'Go into all the world and proclaim the good news to the whole creation.' Mark 16:14-18

One of the most poignant lines in Mark's Gospel for me comes in chapter nine.

'Immediately the father of the child cried out, 'I believe; help my unbelief!' Mark 9:24

I may have read this when I was studying the Bible the first time with a healthy does of cynicism. The full text reads:

'When the whole crowd saw him, they were immediately overcome with awe, and they ran forward to greet him. He asked them, 'What are you arguing about with them?' Someone from the crowd answered him, 'Teacher, I brought you my son; he has a spirit that makes him unable to speak; and whenever it seizes him, it dashes him down; and he foams and grinds his teeth and becomes rigid; and I asked your disciples to cast it out, but they could not do so.' He answered them, 'You faithless generation, how much longer must I be among you? How much longer must I put up with you? Bring him to me.' And they brought the boy to him. When the spirit saw him, immediately it threw the boy into convulsions, and he fell on the ground and rolled about, foaming at the mouth. Jesus asked the father, 'How long has this been happening to him?' And he said, 'From childhood. It has often cast him into the fire and into the water, to destroy him; but if you are able to do anything, have pity on us and help us.' Jesus said to him, 'If you are able!—All things can be done for the one who believes.' Immediately the father of the child cried out, 'I believe; help my unbelief!'

Jesus heals the boy and then consoles the disciples when they ask why they could not drive out the evil spirit. Jesus says, 'This kind can only come out by prayer.'

I believe it is through prayer that we are guided to overcome doubt. Our prayer leads to deeper study of God's word. Deeper study leads to fellowship with others who are seeking God and into a life of serving others instead of ourselves. Amen.

42nd Sunday – Read Luke

'For all who exalt themselves will be humbled, and those who humble themselves will be exalted.' Luke 14:11

January 23, 2011

The Gospel of Jesus Christ according to Luke – It was good for me to read Sharon Ringe's Westminster Bible Companion commentary on Luke this week because some of what she wrote rubbed me the wrong way. This was good because sometimes we get too cozy with the Gospel cherishing our favorites parts and glossing over the hard parts.

For her part in keeping the Gospel rubbing people the wrong way, Hinge brought attention to fact that the Gospels do not represent women in leadership roles very much. This is a sad fact of the time in which Jesus lived. There are plenty of men today who think that women should be in subservient roles in the church and the home and they get their examples from the roles women played back in Bible times. So Ringe has a point but I still couldn't help but think that she overdid it a little. I think the reason that her views are strong is because for me the way the women in the Gospels lived and acted is closer to how I think Christ intended for the men to act but we don't. That is: providing care for others without calling attention to themselves like the woman who anointed Jesus with oil; like the old widow who gave her last two cooper coins to the offering plate; like Mary who sat quietly listening to the teachings of Jesus while everybody else was running around trying to be busy; like the women who were faithfully serving and proclaiming God while the men were hiding out trying to save their own necks.

In Matthew we read that it was the men who deserted Jesus at the time of his greatest need. It was the women who went to care for the burial tomb of Christ and who saw him first. It was the women who first preached the good news that Christ was raised from the dead.

In Luke, we learn a startling fact was well. It was a woman who first confessed belief in Jesus Christ.

Elizabeth exclaimed when the pregnant Mary came to visit 'And why has this happened to me, that the mother of my Lord comes to me?' Luke 1:43

Luke is a beautifully written Gospel that contains a lot of stories not mentioned in the other three. And it's remarkable for demonstrating God's intention to reverse the status quo.

'He has scattered the proud in the thoughts of their hearts. He has brought down the powerful from their thrones, and lifted up the lowly; he has filled the hungry with good things and sent the rich away empty.' 1:51-53

God did indeed send a Messiah to save Israel and the whole world but not with chariots or war horses. God did it through a peasant girl and with a baby who had no place to lay his head.

'And she gave girth to her first-born son and wrapped him in bands of cloth, and laid him in a manager, because there was no place for them in the inn.' Luke 2:7

Why did God do this? We have to understand by now through our reading of the Holy Scriptures and our through own experiences that the world is broken. Recently, I let a man borrow a small amount of money. When he returned the money, he stole something very insignificant from me while smiling to my face. This week I got flustered at my wife because the plumbing contractor didn't immediately follow the tile layers. What is wrong with us?

God knows. We place too much value in our own shrewdness to make things happen when in fact we control very little of what goes on. Everything that we need to live (air, food, communication) comes from God and goes through our airway (into which God first breathed) and yet we do not give God the credit. There is darkness in each of us that has to be overcome. This darkness often manifests itself when we do our best work. Into our gleeful minds, the devil sends thoughts that would make a drunken sailor blush (pride, fantasy mates, and delusional dreams of security (we are like the dog in the commercial that can't sleep because he keeps thinking someone will take his bone.). We also think we are right about everything. And we act like the Glen Close character in the show 'Damages' manipulating good people to get what we want.

It's into this broken world that God became small that we might live. He turned the tables on us. Luke shows in his Gospel how God reversed all that we revere.

The Christ child grew to be a man. He observed how people in positions of power trampled over the poor. He saw how those in charge of the temples played a game of pretending to be pious when inside they were using religious ritual to make themselves look good and keep privilege for themselves

Jesus preached to them and it rubbed them the wrong way, 'Jesus said, 'The Spirit of the Lord is upon me, because he has anointed me to bring good news to the poor. He has sent me to proclaim release to the captives and recovery of sight to the blind, to let the oppressed go free, to proclaim the year of the Lord's favor . . . . When they heard this; all in the synagogue were filled with rage. They got up, drove him out of the town, and led him to the brow of the hill on which their town was built, so that they might hurl him off the cliff. But he passed through the midst of them and went on his way.' Luke 4:18, 28-29

Jesus did not hunker down in the face of this opposition, 'I must proclaim the good news of the kingdom of God to the other cities also; for I was sent for this purpose.' Luke 4:43

When Jesus' disciples first heard him preach, they did not decide to follow him because the worship music was good or because the message was uplifting. No they were convicted by the word of God as Peter exclaimed, 'Go away from me, Lord, for I am a sinful man!' Luke 5:8

And sinners (us all) are who Christ came to serve. 'The Pharisees and their scribes were complaining to his disciples saying, 'Why do you eat with tax collectors and sinners?' Jesus answered, Those who are well have no need of a physician, but those who are sick; I have come to call not the righteous but sinners to repentance.' Luke 5:30-31

Having demonstrated his power from the Holy Spirit to cast out evil and his authority to forgive sins, Jesus teaches us that how we have perceived life heretofore was a lie. Jesus turns our thinking upside down in his famous Sermon on the Mount.

We read the 'blessed be' teachings in Matthew about the poor, the humble and the meek. Luke paints the picture a little clearer / bleaker by adding woes. Ringe: 'The blessing is part of the reversal of fortunes that characterizes God's project, as Luke has already made clear in the hymns and stories of the birth narratives and in the appropriation of the Jubilee text of Isaiah 61:1-2 in Luke 4:18-19. To see the beatitude as rewarding an attitude . . . is to miss the point.'

'Blessed are you who are poor, for yours is the kingdom of God . . . But woe to you who are rich, for you have received your consolation.' Luke 6:20, 24

Ringe: In each case, the blessing makes a statement of fact: one is blessed because of a future that is a sure part of God's reign. There is no threat or challenge in these blessings: Nowhere do they say, 'Do this in order to guarantee a specific result.' They announce a truth about the divine agenda rather than a mandate for human morality . . .

The blessings, in particular, expand on the theme of the good news to the poor, and on such contrasts as prisoners being set free and blind people having their sigh restored. The woes, then, would be a good reason to cause dismay in the townspeople who hear the privileged place in God's project (which they assume belongs to them) being attributed to others.' Luke 4:25-27'

So Jesus preached to change our thinking: love your enemies; bless those who curse you; pray for those who abuse you; be merciful; do not judge.

Jesus said that when you attend a banquet do not sit at the table of honor but sit in a lower place. 'For all who exalt themselves with humbled, and those who humble themselves will be exalted.' He went further saying, by the way when you host a banquet you shouldn't invite the rich and powerful but invite 'the poor the crippled, the lame, and the blind. And you will be blessed, because they cannot repay you . . . ' Luke 14:11, 13 James Howell wrote in 'Exploring Christianity, the Bible, Faith and Life' 'Anyone who says 'I take the Bible literally' ought to shudder over this business about dinner invitations.'

Jesus asks his disciples to consider what they have seen and heard, to compare their life experiences with the message he brought. He asked them, 'Who do you say that I am?' Luke 9:20

God desperately wants us to recognize His divine action in our lives and our dire human situation. Jesus tells a story about two sons. One son wanted to work the land of his father saving his inheritance for the future and one son wanted his reward now. So the father gave the gypsy son his inheritance and sent him on his way. The boy traveled the world and 'squandered his property in dissolute things.' The boy then had to live like a poor person and was so hungry that 'he would gladly have filled himself with the pods the pigs were eating, and no one gave him anything.'

The boy finally was able to get back home. He would be happy if his father let him live like a hired hand. But his father welcomed him back with open arms. The son who had stayed to work the land was not happy about this. The gypsy brother didn't deserve the redemption of his father's love.

But the father said "Son, you are always with me, and all that is mine is yours. But we had to celebrate and rejoice, because this brother of yours was dead and has now come to life; he was lost and has been found.' Luke 15:11-32

God knows. He wants us be saved from living a dissolute life. But we can not be saved from ourselves because we are either the gypsy brother squandering our gifts or we are the loathing brother who doesn't want grace for those undeserving. God knows we are all undeserving.

Jesus gave himself over to all the evil tendencies of man, past, present and future, 'When I was with you day after day in the temple, you did not lay hands of me. But this is your hour, and the power of darkness! Luke 22:53

'When they came to the place that is called The Skull, they crucified Jesus there with the criminals, one on his right side and one on his left. Then Jesus said, 'Father, forgive them; for they do no know what they are doing.' 23:33-34

From our waywardness we are called to be redeemed by Jesus. Nicky Gumbel says we are to start living anew by saying, 'sorry, thank you and please.' We are sorry for living in selfish ways and hurting other people. We are thankful to God for breathing his new life into us. And we say please God; send your Holy Spirit on me that I might live for the kingdom of God now and forever.

We say forever because Jesus did not stay in the tomb. 'While they were talking about this, Jesus himself stood among them and said to them, Peace be with you . . . . While in their joy and disbelieving and still wondering, he said to them. Have you anything here to eat? So they gave him a piece of fish, and he took it and ate in their presence.' Luke 24:36, 41-43

He asked them and he asks us 'Who do you say that I am.' We say My Lord, sorry, thank you, please. Amen

43rd Sunday – Read John

'Sir, give me this water. Sir, give us this bread.'
John 6:34, 4:15

January 30, 2011

The Gospel of Jesus Christ according to John – I remember back when e-mail first became popular. A preacher I knew started sending out faith e-mails. And this preacher encouraged questions. I thought of a good one to ask. Who / what is God? Is God a spirit a force or what? The preacher didn't ever send back long replies. His reply was something like 'sort of.' Exasperated I wrote back in capital letters WHO / WHAT is God? The preacher replied succinctly again but this time stopped me in my tracks. He wrote 'God is love.' I was looking for a long detailed explanation but it didn't take one to relate the truth.

God is love.

We know how to love those close to us and those who do our bidding. But love and justice for those who are not like us is somehow perverted.

"She calls out to the man on the street
'Sir, can you help me?
It's cold and I've nowhere to sleep,
Is there somewhere you can tell me?'
He walks on, doesn't look back
He pretends he can't hear her
Starts to whistle as he crosses the street
Seems embarrassed to be there"

(Phil Collins, 'Another Day in Paradise')

God loves justice.

Heschel though says not equal justice for all, but justice with bias towards the poor. N.T. Wright wrote in 'Simply Christian, Why Christianity Makes Sense' 'We have a sense that justice itself slips through our fingers. Sometimes it works; often it doesn't . . . . People hurt each other badly and walk away laughing . . . The rich use the power of their money to get even richer while the poor, who can't do anything about it, get even poorer. Most of us scratch our heads and wonder why; and then go out and buy another product whose profit goes to the rich company.'

Wright says we know about God's laws but we still break them. 'The line between justice and injustice between things being right and things not being right can't be drawn between 'us' and 'them'. It runs right down through the middle of each one of us. We all know what we ought to do (give or take a few details); but we all manage, at least some of the time, not to do it. Isn't this odd?' Wright asks 'Can the world be rescued? Can we be rescued?'

The author of the book of John thought the world was rescued in Palestine 1,978 years ago. John proclaimed that God himself came down to earth in human form to wallow in our oddness and to show us it doesn't have to be that way. Life can be about love instead of sorrow.

John is one of the most eloquent books in the Bible and one of the most oft quoted for Christians. Bryan Born wrote 'The story seems simple and straightforward, and yet one feels as though the author is often hinting at still deeper truths.'

These deeper truths go all the way back to the first line in the Hebrew Bible. 'In the beginning God created the heavens and the earth.' Genesis 1:1 For Christians this is not just a statement but a deep truth we believe. It provides a foundation for us. We are not just randomly here. God did it. And he did it because he loves us.

John starts his Gospel out with an even deeper truth. 'In the beginning was the Word, and the Word was with God, and the Word was God.' John 1:1 The implication is that Christ was God's first creative act before the foundation of the world.

'This grace was given us in Christ Jesus before this world existed.' 2 Timothy 1:19

'For God so loved the world that he gave his only Son, that whoever believes in him should not perish but have eternal life.' John 3:16

This is the crux of the matter according to Gail O'Day, 'Jesus' life and ministry reveal God's presence to the world, but also confront the world with the difficult decision of whether or not to accept this revelation.'

Will we believe that Christ Jesus is true love and justice?

Awash then in scripture:

'What has come into being in him was life, and the life was the light of all people. The light shines in the darkness, and the darkness did not overcome it.' John 1:4-5

'And the Word became flesh.' John 1:14

'The law came from Moses; grace and truth come through Jesus Christ.' John 1:17

'Here is the Lamb of God who takes away the sin of the world.' John 1:29

Jesus turned water into wine at the wedding in Cana 'and revealed his glory, and his disciples believed in him.' John 2:11

'And this is the judgment, that the light has come into the world, and people loved darkness rather than light . . . ' John 3:19

'Whoever has accepted his testimony has certified this, that God is true.' John 3:33

God is true.

Jesus has a gift for us all. It's living water. To the Samaritan woman Jesus replied, 'If you knew the gift of God, and who it is that is saying to you, Give me a drink, you would have asked him, and he would have given you living water . . . The woman replied, Sir give me this water.' John 4:10, 15

'Jesus said to her, I am He.' John 4:24, 26

When Jesus healed a man who had been ill for 38 years, his earthly troubled started. 'Therefore, the Jews started persecuting Jesus, because he was doing such things on the Sabbath. Jesus answered them, 'My Father is still working, and I also am working.' John 5:16-17

Kierkegaard: 'Wilt thou be offended or wilt thou believe?'

The people came after Jesus asking questions because he performed a sign by feeding five thousand people with five barley loaves and two fish. Jesus said 'You are looking for me, not because you saw signs, but because you ate your fill on loaves. Do not work for food that perishes, but for food that endures for eternal life, which the Son of Man will give you.' They asked 'What must we do to perform the works of God? Jesus answered them; this is the work of God that you believe in him whom he has sent.' John 6 26-29

'For the bread of God is that which comes down from heaven and gives life to the world. They said to him, 'Sir gives us this bread.' John 6:33-34

'Jesus said, I am the bread of life.' John 6:35

'This is indeed the will of my Father that all who see the son and believe in him may have eternal life; and I will raise him up on the last day. John 6:40

'Does this offend you? John 6:60

'I am the light of the world; whoever follows me will never walk in darkness . . . . If you continue in my word, you are truly my disciples, and you will know the truth, and the truth will make you free. Very truly I tell you, before Abraham was, I am.' John 8:12, 31, 58

The blind man said, 'One thing I do know, that though I was blind, now I see.' John 9:25

Jesus said, 'I am the good shepherd. The good shepherd lays down his life for his sheep.' John 10:11

'When Jesus saw her weeping and the Jews who came with her weeping, he was greatly disturbed in spirit and deeply moved . . . . Jesus began to weep.' John 11:33. 35

The Jews said 'If we let him go on like this everyone will believe in him, and the Romans will come and destroy both our holy place, and out nation.' John 11:45

Jesus was flanked by the people during his final entry into Jerusalem. They shouted, 'Hosanna! Blessed is the one who comes in the name of the Lord! John 12:13

Jesus to God, 'Father my soul is troubled . . . but . . . glorify your name . . . The a voice came from heaven, I have glorified it, and I will glorify it again. John 12:27-28

'Now this is the judgment of the world, the ruler of the world will be driven out . . . . For they loved human glory more than the glory that comes from God. ' John 12:31,43

Jesus in final preparation for his death washes the feet of his disciples. He told them to be an example, 'By this everyone will know that you are my disciples if you love one another. John 13:35

Jesus said, you will not be alone when I am gone, 'An Advocate will be with you forever . . . the spirit of truth . . . will abide in you . . . the Advocate / Holy Spirit will teach you everything.' John 14:15-25

'In the world you face persecution, but take courage, I have conquered the world.' John 16:33

In chapter 17, Jesus prayed for us to be protected from the evil one, to be unified and for God to sanctify us in the truth. And not only does Jesus pray for his disciples but for 'those who will believe.' John 17:15, 17, 20

'Mary stood weeping outside the tomb . . . they have taken my Lord and I do not know where they have laid him.' John 20:11, 13

Jesus, 'Mary'
Mary, 'Rabbouni'
Mary, 'I have seen the Lord!'

'Blessed are those who have not seen and yet have come to believe . . . . these are written so that you may come to believe that Jesus is the Messiah, the Son of God, and that through believing you many have life in his name.' John 20:29, 31

Jesus to Peter and the future church,

'Feed my lambs',
'Tend my sheep,'
'Feed my sheep.'

What to do then:

Part of the dinner conversation at our table recently was about the sad situation in Egypt. The majority of the 80 million people who live there are very poor. The Egyptian people see injustice all around them and are standing up to a corrupt government. The government deployed tanks to keep the peace. My youngest daughter simply exclaimed, 'why can't we all just get along.' Less than a half hour later in a telephone conversation with my mother the subject of Egypt came up. Mother exclaimed, 'why can't we all just get along.' Isn't this odd?

For our individual part, perhaps we can't end the conflict in Egypt but we can do something. We can learn to get along with people better like Pope John Paul II did. In his book 'Rise, Let us be on our way,' the beloved Pope wrote about his philosophy in relating to others. He used Jesus as an example. 'The good shepherd knows his sheep and they know him too.' John 10:14

John Paul said we should really get to know the people with whom we come in contact. He said we should 'seek to be close to them, to know about their lives-what gives joy to their hearts and what saddens them.' This type of intimacy comes from developing 'genuine interest in what is happening in their lives regardless of age, social status, or nationality, whether they are close at hand or far away.' John Paul notes there isn't a magic formula for relating with others but a poem by Jerzy Liebert's illustrates one way:

'I study you, my friend,
Slowly I study you, slowly,
This difficult task, its gain,
Brings joy to my heart and pain.'

Another way Pope John Paul found effective for relating to others was through prayer. He said, 'I simply pray for everyone everyday. As soon as I meet people, I pray for them, and this helps me in all my relationships . . . I always follow this principle: I welcome everyone as a person sent to me and entrusted to me by Christ.'

The New Covenant through Christ Jesus calls for his sheep to relentlessly seek love, justice, peace and reconciliation using the Holy Scriptures and a great cloud of witnesses as our guides. Let us pray. Amen.

44th Sunday – Read Acts

'Festus to Paul, "You are out of your mind! Paul to Festus, 'No, I am speaking the sober truth.' Acts 26:24

February 6, 2011

The Acts of the Apostles – After reading about Jesus in volume one, Luke would have been pleased that his friend, 'O lover of God,' had picked up second scroll in the story to read about the birth and works of the early church. So how did the Christian church get started?

Rewind to the upper room the in the days after Jesus' death. His followers were cowered together waiting for the authorities to come and get them. Jesus appeared to them, ate with them and promised them that the Holy Spirit would come upon them and give them courage to teach the world God's message of reconciliation.

'This, he said, is what you have heard from me; for John baptized with water, but you will be baptized with the Holy Spirit not many days from now.' Acts 1:4

Lea Sestieri gives a little background on the Holy Spirit. 'In English copies of the Bible, the word "spirit" occurs about 823 times. Its first occurrence is Genesis 1:2. "Spirit" occurs most often in the Old Testament book Isaiah and the New Testament book Acts. The Hebrew word translated "spirit" or "breath" is ruach. The Greek word is pneuma . . .

The phrase "spirit of God" is reasonably rendered "Breath of God" or "Wind of God." '

Still not clearly understanding the meaning of Christ his friends asked 'Lord is this the time when you will restore the kingdom of Israel? He replied, It is not for you to know the times or periods that the Father has set by his own authority. But you will receive power when the Holy Spirit has come upon you; and you will be my witnesses in Jerusalem, in all Judea and Samaria, and to the ends of the earth.' Acts 1:6-8

And then the RRRRRRUUUUAAAAACH came:

'And suddenly from heaven there came a sound like the rush of a violent wind, and it filled the entire house where they were sitting . . . All of them were filled with the Holy Spirit . . . ' Acts 2:2-4

The crowd reacted 'All were amazed and perplexed, saying to one another, 'What does this mean?' But others sneered and said, 'They are filled with new wine.'

In his Westminster Bible Companion commentary Paul Walaskay writes 'This same God, who breathed the creative breath of life over the face of the deep, has again breathed the divine breath of creation into these Galilean

Jews. . . . Luke emphasizes the importance of the activity of the Holy Spirit in the life of the emerging church. There can be not doubt that the creation of the church is God's creation. God's Spirit, the Holy Spirit, is its life source foundationally and essentially.'

I think we can take comfort from the opening scenes in Acts learning that we do not have to have all the answers. We pray and receive guidance from the Holy Spirit. In our witness, we will encounter all types of reactions. Some will scoff, some will believe and some will say 'not convinced' but tell me more.

As we will see, early followers of Jesus faced Jews, Romans, and Greeks who believed differently that they did. Was it a bed of roses? It seems so at first. Peter who was among the first leaders gave speeches to people in the streets of Jerusalem.

'Now when they heard this, they were cut to the heart and said to Peter and to the other apostles, 'Brothers, what should we do?' Peter said to them, 'Repent, and be baptized every one of you in the name of the Christ so that your sins may be forgiven; and you will receive the gift of the Holy Spirit . . . So those who welcomed his message were baptized, and that day about three thousand persons were added. They devoted themselves to the apostles' teaching and fellowship, to the breaking of bread and prayers.' Acts 2:37-42

'All who believed were together and had all things in common; they would sell their possessions and goods and distribute the proceeds to all, as any had need . . . they broke bread and ate their food with glad and generous hearts, praising God and having the goodwill of all the people.' Acts 2:43-47

Luke seems to be giving us a glimpse of how things might be. Fresh with power from the Holy Spirit, believers shared with one another as the Apostles preached, healed and performed many signs and wonders. But this peaceful easy feeling didn't last long.

'While Peter and John were speaking to the people, the priests, the captain of the temple, and the Sadducees came to them, much annoyed because they were teaching the people and proclaiming that in Jesus there is resurrection of the dead. So they arrested them and put them in custody.' Acts 4:1-3

Peter and John do not back down from the authorities. 'We cannot keep from speaking about what we have seen and heard.' Peter and John were released from jail and they prayed with their followers. 'When they had prayed, the place in which they were gathered was shaken; and they were all filled with the Holy Spirit and spoke the word of God with boldness.' Acts 4; 20, 31

Walaskay: The council was amazed by the level of conversation conducted by these 'uneducated and ordinary men.' Perhaps members of the council presumed that ignorant fisherman would always remain so.'

The apostles were arrested again. The authorities said 'We gave you strict orders not to teach in this name . . . Peter responded, 'We must obey God rather than any human author. The God of our ancestors raised up Jesus, who you had killed by hanging him on a tree. God exalted him at his right hand as Leader and Savior that he might give repentance to Israel and forgiveness of sins. And we are witnesses to these things, and so is the Holy Spirit who God has given to those who obey him.' The apostles were flogged and ordered not to speak anymore. 'They rejoiced that there were considered worthy to suffer dishonor for the sake of the name. And every day in the temple and at home they did not cease to teach and proclaim Jesus as the Messiah.' Acts 5:17-42

At this point in the story there was 'Kum ba yah' no more. Things turned really ugly when Stephen was stoned to death. Stephen preached the gospel mightily, 'When they heard these things, they became enraged and ground their teeth at Stephen . . . And Saul approved of their killing him. Acts 7:54, 8:1

'That day a severe persecution began against the church . . . . Devout men buried Stephen and made loud lamentations over him. But Saul was ravaging the church by entering house after house; dragging off both men and women, he committed them to prison. Acts 8:1-3

Some of the faithful like Philip left Jerusalem to proclaim the word in other places. 'Then and angel of the Lord said to Phillip, Get up and go . . . So he got up and went.' Acts 8:26-27

Walasky: 'In fine Old Testament fashion and angel of the Lord came to Philip with traveling orders.'

And it was at this point that Jerusalem could no longer contain God's word. God would use who he chose. He chose Saul.

"Meanwhile Saul was still breathing threats and murder against the disciples of the Lord . . . when suddenly a light from heaven flashed around him. He fell to the ground and heard a voice saying to him, 'Saul, why do you persecute me?' He asked, 'Who are you, Lord?' The reply came, 'I am Jesus . . . get up and you will be told what to do.' Acts 9:1-6

Saul was stuck blind on the road to Damascus. God sent a devout man Ananias to heal him. 'Brother Saul, the Lord Jesus, who appeared to you on your way here, has sent me so that you may regain your sight and be filled with the Holy Spirit . . . Saul got up was baptized . . . and immediately began to proclaim Jesus in the synagogues, saying 'He is the Son of God.' Acts 9:1-22

Saul, whose roman name is Paul is now an advocate for 'The Way.'

Walaskay speaks at length in his commentary about Saul's background as an educated Roman Pharisee. He asks a fairly common question at this point. Was Saul converted by what he had heard or was he really called by God?

Walasky: Paul's problem was a universal one; he is mortal-a member of the human race with all its built-in limitations. Sin is the universal human condition that needs to be addressed on a universal scale. Only God can do this . . . . What contemporary readers do see in the Damascus road experience, from the perspective of both Paul and Luke, is a call from God. Rather than a negative 'turn your back on the past,' Paul received a positive 'turn you face toward the future . . . In doing this, we, like Paul, enter the process of completing God's joy by expanding God's love in the world. And as we reflect on experience, we like Paul, -come to discover that God was there all along; transforming destructive anger into overflowing joy.'

Saul preached the Word about the Way. Pretty soon the Jews started trying to kill him too. When the apostles heard about this they sent him off to Tarsus to spread the good news.

This business of speaking words and ideas contrary to the popular notions of the day was dangerous business. Luke reports a little more about the work of the original apostles including a story about Peter and Cornelius who was a Gentile.

Walaskay: 'Here is Peter, a fisherman from Galilee, claiming that he now knows, because of a dream and his interpretation of it that God has changed a millennium of divinely ordered regulations regarding social interactions between Jews and Gentiles.'

'Then Peter began to speak to them: 'I truly understand that God shows no partiality, but in every nation anyone who fears him and does what is right is acceptable to him . . . . he is Lord of all. Acts 10:34-36

Peter preached and offended. He slips in and out of prison and we do not hear much about him again in Acts. 'But the word of God continued to advance and gain adherents.' Acts 12:24

The rest of Acts focuses on Paul and his missionary journeys to the Gentiles of the world. In one synagogue speaking to a Jewish audience, Paul said 'Since you reject it and judge yourselves to be unworthy of eternal life, we are now turning to the Gentiles. For so the Lord commanded us, saying, I have set you to be a light for the Gentiles so that you may bring salvation to the ends of the earth.' Acts 13:46-47

In the rest of the book, a pattern will emerges. Paul preaches and some people will believe. The power brokers get mad and run Paul and his companions out of town.

'Then the Gentiles heard this, they were glad and praised the word of the Lord; and as many as had been destined for eternal life became believers . . . . But . . . Jews stirred up persecution against Paul and Barnabas, and drove them out of their region. Acts 13:48-50

'But the residents of the city were divided; some sided with the Jews and some with the apostles.' Acts 14:4

Paul went to Asia Minor, Greece and Italy. He visited towns called Ephesus, Colossae, Corinth, Philippi, Thessalonica and Rome.

False God or idols have always been a big problem in the Bible. The towns Paul visited were no exception except some of the God they worshipped may be more familiar to us.

In one town, Paul healed a man and the crowd went wild. They call Barnabas, Zeus and Paul, Hermes. Paul replies 'Friends, why are you doing this? We are mortals just like you, and we bring you good news, that you should turn from these worthless things to the living God, who made the heaven and the earth and the sea and all that is in them. Acts 14:15

As Jews, Paul and his companions were confounded about what to do about the rituals and regulations of the Jewish faith especially with fresh believers who did not know the history of these things. So there was a big meeting back in Jerusalem that could be described as the first Christian council. The main topic was about circumcision. Jesus' brother James appears to have had the most standing among the early followers and he made the final call.

'James replied, my brothers, listen to me . . . I have reached the decision that we should not trouble those Gentiles who are turning to God.' Acts 15:19

After the council meeting, Paul and Barnabas go back out for their second missionary work. 'Come, let us return and visit the believers in every city where we proclaimed the word of the Lord and see how they are doing.' Acts 15:36

Paul and his new companion Silas got arrested again and were flogged. They got out of jail and went to another city saying 'This is the Messiah, Jesus whom I am proclaiming to you. Some of them were persuaded and joined Paul and Silas, as did a great many of the devout Greeks and not a few of the leading women. But the Jews became jealous, and with the help of some ruffians in the marketplace they formed a mob and set the city in an uproar.' Acts 17:3-5

Paul went next to Athens and met with some Epicureans and Stoics. 'Some said, 'What does this babbler want to say . . . we would like to know what it means.'

Paul 'To an unknown god, what therefore you worship as unknown, this I proclaim to you . . . . the God who made the world . . . is not a deity like gold or sliver or stone, and image formed by art and imagination or mortals . . . . when they heard of the resurrection of the dead, some scoffed, but others said, we want to hear you again about this. Acts 17

Walaskay: The phrase 'To an unknown god' 'provided Paul with a text for interpretation and discussion that reminds the reader that Paul is far removed from the world of the Bible. '

Paul is accused again by some such and such figure in charge. 'If it were a matter of crime or serious villainy, I would be justified in accepting the complaint of the Jews, but since it is a matter about words and names and your own law, see to it yourselves.' Acts 18

Paul began his third and final missionary journey. It would take him to new places and he would revisit some of the churches he had planted. Finally he will end up in Rome.

'He entered the synagogue and for three months spoke out boldly, and argued persuasively about the kingdom of God. When some stubbornly refused to believe and spoke evil of the Way before the congregation, he left them, taking the disciples with him, and argued daily in the lecture hall of Tyrannus. This continued for two years, so that all the residents of Asia, both Jews and Greeks, heard the word of the Lord. Acts 19:8-10

'About that time no little disturbance broke out concerning the Way . . . a silversmith who made silver shrines of Artemis brought no little business to the artisans.' In other words the folks that made their money off of figurine Gods were getting ticked off. The massive crowds shouted in unison 'Great is Artemis of the Ephesians!' Acts 19

Paul is arrested for what looks like the last time. Paul gets to trial and retorts, "It is about the resurrection of the dead that I am on trial before you today. Acts 24:21 'Festus exclaimed, 'You are out of your mind, Paul! Too much learning is driving you insane.' But Paul said, I am not out of my mind, most excellent Festus, but I am speaking the sober truth.' Acts 26:24-25

Paul was finally sent to Rome where he requested to be judged by the emperor. After a perilous ship voyage Paul arrives in the ancient city. Luke does not report the about the trial or what ultimately became of Paul. We also are not told about the fate of the other Apostles.

Walaskay: Perhaps, like a good storyteller, Luke concluded the story knowing that all of these questions, and more, would be left unresolved. If he has drawn us in and piqued our interest about the Christian church, he has done his job . . . Luke might have imagined that those who read his history would be traveling their own segment of the sacred journey, and they would write their own continuation of the story.'

Would it be that as 'Lover's of God' we did steady and sure works in His name.

45th Sunday – Read Romans

'For all who are led by the Spirit of God are children of God.' Romans 8:14

February 13, 2011

Romans – When we read the book of Romans, we are reading someone else's mail. The Epistles in the New Testament are letters sent by the Apostles to a certain church community. The letters were often addressing specific concerns; concerns about doctrine if you will. This letter was written by Paul to a Christian community in Rome, one that he had not yet visited. At one time or another in our lives, we have all probably saved a letter. Isn't it cool that an ancient Roman church saved this one for us?

It is interesting that the letter Paul wrote to the Romans was written before the Gospels. While Paul may have been aware of the oral testimony of the Gospels it is unlikely he had them in written form. So Paul is fleshing out what it means to him to be a Christian. Many new Christian communities had Jewish roots. Some wanted to know what they were to do about the laws and rituals of the Hebrew Scriptures. Other new communities had people do things that seemed, well unchristian. So the letters addressed some of those issues.

Throughout the history of biblical academia, Paul has had his share of critics. Some have used his writing to support crazed notions such as believing that the Jewish religion is false. Others have simply used his writing to codify their own misguided notions of Christianity like women not having a role in the church. But by and large, Paul is a treated a huge literary figure and well respected.

That Paul was a huge influence can be supported by the effect his writing had on important Christian figures of the past such as Augustine, Martin Luther, Karl Barth and John Wesley. Each of these giants had major conversion experiences while reading Paul's letter to the Romans.

One last point before examining the text is that we do not always know the exact questions Paul was addressing in his letters. We may not always be correct in assuming we understand the point he makes by reading a particular verse. It is important therefore, to read the letter as a whole body of work.

In his Westminster Bible Companion Commentary, David Bartlett helps us get a since of the purpose of Paul's letter to the Romans. He writes, 'The claim that in Jesus Christ God does what is right for the whole creation, is at the heart of the letter to the Christians at Rome . . . Paul writes Romans to affirm and expand the central claim of his Jewish tradition: the Lord God is one.'

'Or is God the God of Jews only? Is he not the God of Gentiles also? Yes, of Gentiles also.' Romans 3:29

Bartlett also says that Paul claimed, "The one God has determined a way by which to stake God's claim over all people, through the cross and resurrection of Jesus Christ, Christ is God's gift, not just for one group but for all humankind. The way in which all of humankind-of whatever nationality or religion- can acknowledge God's claim is through faith in the one person Jesus Christ.'

This summation raises thorny issues. There is so much division in the Christian church today with each denomination thinking it has a corner on the truth (much like each one of us individually). Bartlett: "There is also a harder question. Is God the God of Christians only?'

The letter then: 'To all God's beloved in Rome, who are called to be saints; Grace and peace from God our Father and the Lord Jesus Christ.' Romans 1:7

I am reminded here of a quotation from Charles Peguy. He wrote "life holds only one tragedy, ultimately: not to have been a saint."

Paul continues, "I am not ashamed of the gospel; it is the power of God for salvation to everyone who has faith, to the Jew first and also to the Greek. For in it the righteousness of God is revealed through faith for faith; as it is written: The one who is righteous will live by faith.' Romans 1:16-17 (Paul is quoting the prophet Habakkuk 2:4)

Bartlett: 'Through faith in the one God we are spared the depressing possibility that we might be it, the final creator of our own goods and goals, the only god we've got . . . Through faith we place our trust in the righteous God, knowing that, in Jesus Christ, God also makes us right, for now and for eternity.'

Paul builds his case for Christ by pointing out what we have known since the beginning of the Bible and that is the sinful nature of man. 'For though they knew God, they did not honor him as God or give him thanks, but they became futile in their thinking . . . exchanging the truth about God for a lie.' Romans 1:21, 25

Charles Peguy again, "At the heart of Christianity is the sinner.'

Paul chastises us for judging others when we do the very same things we are commending in others. Bartlett: "In our churches, denominations, families, and other relationships the temptation is to see what's wrong with everyone else and ignore what's wrong with us.'

"And if you are sure that you are a guide to the blind, a light to those who are in darkness, a corrector of the foolish, a teacher of children, having in the law the embodiment of knowledge and truth, you then, that teach others, will you not teach yourself?' Romans 2:19-21

Oh my.

'What then? Are we any better off? No, not at all, for we have already charged that all, both Jew and Greeks, are under the power of sin . . . . all have sinned and fall short of the glory of God' Romans 3:9, 23

Paul continues building his case for faith by using Abraham as an example. 'No distrust made him waver concerning the promise of God, but he grew strong is his faith as he gave glory to God, being fully convinced that God was able to do what he had promised. Therefore, his faith was reckoned to him as righteousness. Now the words, 'it was reckoned to him,' were written not for his sake alone, but for ours also. It will be reckoned to us who believe in him who raised Jesus our Lord from the dead, who was handed over to death for our trespasses and was raised for our justification.' Romans 4:20-25

'Therefore, since we are justified by faith, we have peace with God, through our Lord Jesus Christ, through whom we have obtained access to this grace in which we stand; and we boast in our hope of sharing the glory of God. And not only that, but we also boast in our sufferings, knowing that suffering produces endurance, and endurance produces character and character produces hope, and hope does not disappoint us, because God's love has been poured into our hearts through the Holy Spirit that has been given to us.' Romans 5:1-5

Justification, faith, grace, hope and glory! These are mighty Christian words!

Bartlett on Christian hope: 'The hope of a person with integrity is not simply the cheery belief that all's for the best despite all evidence to the contrary. The hope of a person of integrity is the hope that emerges because that person has lived through the worst and not lost faith.' Bartlett shares an anonymous poem:

'If but one message I may leave behind,
One single word of comfort for my kind,
It would be this,
O brother, sister, friend,
Whatever life may bring or God may send,
Take heart and wait.

Despair may tangle darkly at your feet
And hope once cool and sweet be lost.
But suddenly above a hill
A heavenly lamp set on heavenly sill
Will shine for you
And point the way to go

How well I know,
For I have waited through the dark,
And I have seen a star rise in the blackest sky, repeatedly,
It has not failed me yet,
And I have learned

God will never forget
To light his lamp.
If we but wait for it,
It will be lit.'

'Therefore, just as one man's trespass led to condemnation for all, so one man's act of righteousness leads to justification and life for all.' Romans 5:18

Bartlett: 'Adam represents disobedience, which leads to condemnation. Jesus Christ represents obedience, which leads to justification and life.'

Paul goes to great lengths to illustrate the human condition. People can try and keep the law perfectly but they can't do it.

'Yet, if it had not been for the law, I would not have known sin. I would not have known what it is to covet if the law had not said, 'You shall not covet.' But sin, seizing an opportunity in the commandment, produced in me all kinds of covetousness.'

'I do not understand my own actions. For I do not do what I want, but I do the very thing I hate . . . . For I do not do the good I want, but the evil I do not want is what I do . . . For I delight in the law of God in my inmost self, but I am captive to the law of sin that dwells in my members. Wretched man that I am! Who will rescue me from this body of death? Thanks be to God through Jesus Christ our Lord! Romans 7:7-25

Bartlett reminds us that when we read the 'I' Paul is using in chapter seven we would do well to insert 'we' into our reading.

At this point Paul showed the Romans that life under the law had ended and a new age had begun. It was a life in the Spirit.

'For the law of the Spirit of life in Christ Jesus has set you free from the law of sin and death. For God has done what the law, weakened by the flesh, could not do: by sending his own Son in the likeness of sinful flesh, and to deal with sin, he condemned sin in the flesh.' Romans 8:1-3

'We know that the whole creation has been groaning in labor pains until now . . . but we ourselves groan inwardly while we wait for adoption, the redemption of our bodies. For in hope we are saved . . . Likewise the Spirit helps us in our weakness; for we do not know how to pray as we ought, but that very Spirit intercedes with sighs too deep for words. Romans 8:22-26

'What then are we to say about these things? . . . It is Christ Jesus, who died, yes, who was raised, who is at the right hand of God who indeed intercedes for us. Who will separate us from the love of Christ? Romans 8:31,34

'Because if you confess with your lips that Jesus is Lord and believe in your heart that God raised him from the dead, you will be saved . . . The scripture says, 'No one who believes in him will be put to shame. For there is no distinction between Jew and Greek; the same Lord is Lord of all and is generous who call on him. For everyone who calls on the name of the Lord shall be saved. Romans 10:9-13

In the final chapters of Romans Paul seems to be answering some of the unspecified concerns he had heard about in Rome. Bartlett: 'What Paul has heard of the Roman churches suggests that they are not of one voice but of many. They do not live together as God's people but in divisions.'

'I appeal to you therefore, brothers and sisters, by the mercies of God, to present your bodies as a living sacrifice, holy and acceptable to God, which is your spiritual worship. Do not be conformed to this world, but be transformed by the renewing of your minds, so that you may discern what is the will of God-what is good and acceptable and perfect. For by the grace given to me I say to everyone among you not to think of yourself more highly that you ought to think, but to think with sober judgment, each according to the measure of faith that God has assigned.'

'Let love be genuine, hate what is evil, hold fast to what is good; love one another with mutual affection, outdo one another is showing honor. Do not lag in zeal, be ardent in spirit, serve the Lord, Rejoice in hope, be patient in suffering, persevere in prayer.' Romans 12:1-12

'Bless those who persecute you . . . rejoice with those who rejoice, weep with those who weep. Live in harmony with one another; do not be haughty; but associate with the lowly; do not claim to be wiser than you are . . . If possible, so far as it depends on you, live peaceably with all.' Romans 12:14-18

'Besides this, you know what time it is, how it is now the moment for you to wake you from sleep. For salvation is nearer to us now that when we became believers; the night is far gone, the day is near. Let us then lay aside the works of darkness and put on the armor of light.' Romans 13:11-12

'For the kingdom of God is not food and drink but righteousness and peace and joy in the Holy Spirit . . . . Let us then pursue what makes for peace and for mutual upbuilding.' Romans 14:17, 19

'We who are strong ought to put up with the failings of the weak and not please ourselves . . . for Christ did not please himself, but, as it is written, 'The insults of those who insult you have fallen on me.'

'May the God of steadfastness and encouragement grant you to live in harmony with one another, in accordance with Christ Jesus so that together you may with one voice glorify the God and Father of our Lord Jesus Christ. May the God of hope fill you with all joy and peace in believing, so that you may abound in hope by the power of the Holy Spirit.' Romans 15:1-13

We may have many unanswered questions after reading Romans. But we get a sense of how life for the Christian church was to be different than temple worship. The Christian ideology of grace abounding will put us toward right thinking about our questions if we practice grace ourselves. So how will we talk with others about Christ Jesus?

Bartlett: 'One way to talk about what God has done in Jesus Christ is for the church to declare God's welcome to every human being. There are no dues you have to pay to know God's love, no hoops to jump through to enter into God's presence, no steps to climb, no set rules of have to obey before God's arms will open. God has run down the steps from the porch and down the road to welcome each one of us as we come home penitent from the far country, and to welcome every last one of our brothers and sisters, too.'

46th Sunday – Read 1 and 2 Corinthians

'Yes, everything is for your sake, so that grace, as it extends to more and people, may increase thanksgiving to the glory of God.' 2 Cor 4:15

February 20, 2011

1 and 2 Corinthians – In these letters, Paul is trying to head off trouble in Corinth. The church is in an uproar about deciding to whom its allegiance belongs. Some are engaging in immoral acts. Church members are suing

one another. Other people are making a mockery of the Lord's Supper and using spiritual gifts as a means to show themselves as enlightened. There were even people in the church denying the resurrection of Christ. I think these books are dangerous to be read casually for this reason, Paul picks his battles carefully.

'And so brothers and sisters, I could not speak to you as spiritual people, but rather as people of flesh, as infants in Christ. I fed you with milk, not with solid food, for you were not ready for solid food. Even now you are still not ready.' 1 Cor 3:1-2

For example, some issues regarding women are were glossed over by Paul. Today we would read his stance towards women as derogatory. Paul does not take a stand against those in Corinth who would have women cover their heads and keep silent in church. But within the larger context, there were more immediate battles to be fought by Paul. When they were ready for solid food he might have given different guidance on these matters. This might be so because Paul corresponded with women and always greeted his brothers and sisters in Christ. To wit:

'For it has been reported to me by Chloe's people that there are quarrels among you, my brothers and sisters. What I mean is that each of you says, 'I belong to Paul, or I belong to Apollos, or I belong to Cephas, or I belong to Christ. Has Christ been divided? 1 Cor 1:11-13

If this weren't so serious it would be funny. The church had barely begun when the quarreling started. One group inside the church thinks it knows best. Humans begin creating their turf. They side with the folks whose ideas suits them best. It is exactly the same way today. People want to run churches with the wisdom of the world. Paul calls this folly.

'God chose what is weak in the world to shame the wise; God chose what is weak in the world to shame the strong; God chose what is low and despised in the world, things that are not, to reduce to nothing things that are, so that no none might boast in the presence of God.' 1 Cor 1:27-29

Paul humbles himself.

'I did not come proclaiming the mystery of God to you in lofty words or wisdom. For I decided to know nothing among you except Jesus Christ, and him crucified . . . . so that your faith might not rest on human wisdom but on the power of God. ' 1 Cor 2:1-5

Paul tried to correct the matter about who is the right leader to follow.

'I planted, Apollos watered, but God gave the growth.' 1 Cor 3:6

'So let no one boast about human leaders . . . you belong to Christ and Christ belongs to God. 1 Cor 3:21-23

'It is actually reported that there is sexual immorality among you, and of a kind that is not found even among the pagans; for a man is living with his father's wife . . . . Drive out the wicked person from among you' 1 Cor 5 1,13

'When has any of you has a grievance against another do you dare to take it to court before the unrighteous, instead of taking it before the saints? Can it be that there is no one among you wise enough to decide between on believer and another, but a believer goes to courts against a believer-and before unbelievers at that? Why not rather be wronged?

Do not be deceived! Fornicators, idolaters, adulterers, male prostitutes, sodomites, thieves, the greedy, drunkards, revilers, robbers, not of these will inherit the kingdom of God. And this is what some of you used to be. But you were washed, you were sanctified, you were justified in the name of the Lord Jesus Christ and in the Spirit of God.' 1 Cor 6

Paul goes on to speak on issues of marriage. There must have been some bizarre views developed by some in the Corinth church. Some thought that since they were forgiven by Christ they could do anything they wanted sexually (many false prophets over the years have claimed the dirty nature of the body and it was only the spiritual life that mattered). Others went to the opposite extreme claiming that total asceticism and chastity was the only way to go.

'Let each of you lead the life that the Lord has assigned, to which God called you.'

Paul then has to issue a lecture to a group that has been eating food that had been sacrificed in the temples to idols.

'Food will not bring us close to God . . . Therefore my friends; flee from the worship of idols. I speak as to sensible people judge for yourselves what I say. The cup of blessing that we bless, is it not a sharing in the blood of Christ? The bread that we break, is it not a sharing of the body of Christ

'I imply that what pagans sacrifice, they sacrifice to demons and not to God. I do not want to be partners with demons. You cannot drink of the cup of the Lord and the cup of demons . . . So, whether you eat or drink, or whatever you do, do everything for the glory of God.' 1 Cor 10:14-31

In chapter 11 Paul admonishes the rich folks in church for having a lavish 'Lord's Supper' meal at church while some church members had little to eat.

'For I received from the Lord what I also handed on to you, that the Lord Jesus on the night when he was betrayed took a loaf of bread, and when he had given thanks, he broke it and said, 'This is my body that is for you. Do this in remembrance of me.' In the same way he took the cup also, after supper, saying, 'This cup is the new covenant in my blood. Do this, as often as you drink it, in remembrance of me.' For as often as you eat this bread and drink the cup, you proclaim the Lord's death until he comes.'

'Whoever therefore eats the bread or drinks the cup of the Lord in an unworthy manner will be answerable for the body and the blood of the Lord. Examine yourselves, and only then eat of the bread and drink of the cup.'

'So then, brothers and sisters, when you come together to eat, wait for one another. If you are hungry, eat at home, so that when you come together it will not be for your condemnation.' 1 Cor 11

And there was the lot in the church who thought they had all these mighty spiritual gifts. It looks to Paul like they are using them to call attention to themselves and to promote false practices.

"Now concerning spiritual gifts . . . I want you to understand that no one speaking by the Spirit of God ever says, 'Let Jesus be cursed!' And no one can say 'Jesus is lord except by the Holy Spirit.' 1 Cor 12:1

'I will show you a still more excellent way. If I speak in the tongues of mortals and of angels but do not have love, I am a noisy gong or a clanging symbol. 1 Cor 13:1

Pursue love and strive for the spiritual gifts, and especially that you may prophesy. For the those who speak in tongue do not speak to other people but to God, for nobody understands them . . . Those who speak in tongues build up themselves, but those who prophesy build up the church. 1 Cor 14

It is really all about the resurrected Christ.

'Now I would remind you, brother and sisters of the good news . . . that Christ died for our sins in accordance with the scriptures, and that he was buried, and that he was raised on the third day in accordance with scriptures, and that he appeared to Cephas, then to the twelve. Then he appeared to more than five hundred brothers and sisters at one time, most of whom are still alive, though some have died. Then he appeared to James, then to all the apostles. Last of all, as to someone untimely born, he appeared also to me. For I am the least of the apostles, unfit to be called an apostle, because I persecuted the church of God. But by the grace of God I am what I am, and his grace towards me has not been in vain.'

'Now if Christ is proclaimed as raised from the dead, how can some you say there is no resurrection of the dead? . . . If for this life only we have hoped in Christ, we are of all people most to be pitied. 1 Cor 15

'Therefore, me beloved, be steadfast, immovable always excelling in the work of the Lord . . . keep alert, stand firm in your faith, be courageous, be strong. Let all that you do be done in love . . . . The grace of the Lord Jesus be with you. 1 Cor 16

That there is a second letter to the Corinthians indicates that the dialogue between Paul and the church was a work in progress. We might imagine that the church had written back Paul after it received the first letter asking for clarification on some matters. It might have been that Paul visited the church in person after the first letter and found that all was not well. Further instruction needed to be provided. In all likelihood things were worse than this. Paul's authority to teach was being called into question by what Paul refers to as 'false apostles.' So Paul defended himself to those who challenged his authority.

In the beginning of 2 Corinthians, Paul sets the tone of his defense by speaking about suffering and affliction. The road for planting churches was filled with potholes. Paul will speak vividly about this latter.

'Indeed, we felt that we had received the sentence of death so that we would rely not on ourselves but on God who raises the dead.' 2 Cor 1:9

Paul also noted that is was in community that he had the strength to continue to build churches.

'As you also join in helping us by your prayers, so that many will give thanks on our behalf for the blessing granted us through the prayers of many.' 2 Cor 1:11

Paul reminds the Corinthians that it is 'with frankness and godly sincerity' that he preached to them. On whatever matters there has been disagreement Paul urged forgiveness.

'Anyone whom you forgive, I also forgive . . . . And we do this so that we may not be outwitted by Satan; for we are not ignorant of his designs.' 2 Cor 2:10-11

And we start to get at the point of those challenging his authority.

"For we are not peddlers of God's word like so many but in Christ we speak as persons of sincerity, as persons sent from God and standing in his presence. 2 Cor 2:17

Paul is such a great user of rhetoric.

'Surely we do not need a letter, as some do, letters of recommendation to you or from you do we? You yourselves are our letters written on our hearts, to be known and read by all, and you show that you are a letter of Christ, prepared by us, written not in ink but with the Spirit of the living God, not on tablets of stone, but on tablets of human hearts. 2 Cor 3:1-3

Paul makes another big point against those who puff themselves up.

'For we do not proclaim ourselves we proclaim Jesus Christ as Lord and ourselves as your slaves for Jesus' sake. 2 Cor 4:5

Paul said that he had not been sitting around like a fat cat orating fancifully.

'We are afflicted in every way, but not crushed; perplexed, but not driven to despair; persecuted, but not forsaken, struck down, but not destroyed; always carrying in the body the death of Jesus, so that the life of Jesus may also be made visible in our bodies. 2 Cor 8-10

Paul is fleshing out in Christian life the theology of the cross.

'Yes, everything is for your sake, so that grace, as it extends to more and more people, may increase thanksgiving to the glory of God.' 2 Cor 4:15

Whether we know it or not; whether we believe it or not we were made to give glory to God.

'And he for all, so that those who live might live no longer for themselves, but for him who died and was raised for them. 2 Cor 5:15

'All this is from God who reconciled us to himself through Christ, and has given to us the ministry of reconciliation; that is, in Christ God was reconciling the world to himself, not counting their trespasses against them, and entrusting the message of reconciliation to us. So we are ambassadors for Christ.' 2 Cor 5:18-20

In the letter Paul reminded the Corinthians again about the collection. "Each of you must give as you have made up your mind, not reluctantly or under compulsion, for God loves a cheerful giver. And God is able to provide you with every blessing in abundance so that by always having enough of everything, you may share abundantly in every good work. 2 Cor 9:7-8

The letter reaches its climax in chapters 10-12.

'I myself, Paul, appeal to you by the meekness and gentleness of Christ- I whom am humble . . . do not show boldness by daring to oppose those who think we are acting according to human standards. Indeed, we live as human beings, but we do not wage war according to human standards; for the weapons of our warfare are not merely human; but they have divine power to destroy strongholds. 2 Cor 10:1-4

'I wish you would bear with me in a little foolishness . . . I am afraid that as the serpent deceived Eve by its cunning, your thoughts will be led astray from a sincere and pure devotion to Christ. For if someone comes and proclaims another Jesus than the one we proclaimed, or if you receive a different spirit from the one you receive, or a different gospel from the one you accepted, you submit to it readily enough. I think that I am not in the least inferior to these super-apostles. I may be untrained in speech, but not in knowledge certainly in every way and in all things we have made evident to you.

'Did I commit a sin by humbling myself so that you might be exalted, because I proclaimed God's good news to you free of charge!

And what I do I will also continue to do, in order to deny an opportunity to those who want an opportunity to be recognized as our equals in what they boast about. For such boasters are false apostles, deceitful workers, disguising themselves as apostles of Christ. And no wonder! Even Satan disguises himself as an angel of light.' 2 Cor 11

In a crescendo Paul asks his followers to compare his deeds to the deeds of the false apostles.

'But whatever anyone dares to boast of—I am speaking as a fool—I also dare to boast of that. Are they Hebrews? So am I. Are they Israelites? So am I. Are they descendants of Abraham? So am I. Are they ministers of Christ? I am talking like a madman—I am a better one: with far greater labors, far more imprisonments, with countless floggings, and often near death. Five times I have received from the Jews the forty lashes minus one. Three times I was beaten with rods. Once I received a stoning. Three times I was shipwrecked; for a night and a day I was adrift at sea; on frequent journeys, in danger from rivers, danger from bandits, danger from my own people, danger from Gentiles, danger in the city, danger in the wilderness, danger at sea, danger from false brothers and sisters; in toil and hardship, through many a sleepless night, hungry and thirsty, often without food, cold and naked. And, besides other things, I am under daily pressure because of my anxiety for all the churches. Who is weak, and I am not weak? Who is made to stumble, and I am not indignant?

If I must boast, I will boast of the things that show my weakness. The God and Father of the Lord Jesus (blessed be he for ever!) knows that I do not lie.' 2 Cor 11

One of the most compelling lines in scripture comes in chapter 12. As Paul concludes his defense of his authority to teach the gospel of the risen Christ he mentions a problem that he has. Many have opinions but no one knows what it was. Paul has just told the Corinthians about visions that he has had.

'I . . . was caught up into Paradise and heard things that are not to be told, that no mortal is permitted to repeat.' 2 Cor 12:4

Therefore, to keep me from being too elated, a thorn was given to me in the flesh, a messenger of Satan to torment me, to keep me from being too elated. Three times I appealed to the Lord about this, that it would leave me, but he said to me, 'My grace is sufficient for you, for power is made perfect in weakness.' So, I will boast all the more gladly of my weaknesses, so that the power of Christ may dwell in me. Therefore I am content with weaknesses, insults, hardships, persecutions, and calamities for the sake of Christ; for whenever I am weak, then I am strong. 2 Cor 12:7-10

Then . . . 'I am not at all inferior to these super-apostles, even though I am nothing . . . . Everything we do, beloved, is for building you up . . . examine yourselves to see whether you are living in the faith. Test yourselves. Do you not realize the Jesus Christ is in you?

Put things in order, listen to my appeal, agree with on another, live in peace, and the God of love and peace will be with you. The grace of the Lord Jesus Christ, the love of God, and the communion of the Holy Spirit be with all of you. 2 Cor 13

47th Sunday – Read Galatians, Ephesians, Philippians

'Live as children of light-for the fruit of the light is found in all that is good and right and true. Try and find out what is pleasing to the Lord.' Eph 5:9-10

February 27, 2011

Galatians, Ephesians, Philippians – Paul's churches were on fire. He planted churches by proclaiming to them the gospel of Christ Jesus but when he left other people came into the fold and twisted the message. For the church in Galatia, it appeared that believers with Jewish backgrounds came and told the people they were welcome to follow Christ but they had to become circumcised and follow the Jewish law in order to do this properly. Since the letters in the New Testament are not listed in the canon in chronological order, we've already learned by reading the book of Acts and Paul's letters to the Romans that a ruling was made by James at the Jerusalem council that the Gentiles did not have to be circumcised.

'Therefore, I have reached the decision that we should not trouble those Gentiles who are turning to God, but we should write to them to abstain only from things polluted by idols and from fornication and from whatever has been strangled and from blood.' Acts 15:19-20

Even though James added a few prohibitions, he certainly did not list all 633 laws that the Jews were supposed to follow. Paul took this to mean that following the Jewish law was not a requirement for being a Christian. And that is what he taught.

'To the churches of Galatia:

Grace to you and peace from God our Father and the Lord Jesus Christ . . . I am astonished that you are so quickly deserting the one who called you in the grace of Christ and are turning to a different gospel- not that there is a another gospel, but there are some who are confusing you and want to pervert the gospel of Christ.' Galatians 1:2-7

'As we have said before, so now I repeat, if anyone proclaims to you a gospel contrary to what you received, let that one be accursed. Galatians 1:9

I have recently become attracted to the television show 'Damages.' In the final episodes of season one, the young attorney Ellen Parsons witnessed the deaths of three people as the trial she was working on reached its climax. One of the deaths was her own fiancée. Long story short, Parsons decided not to quit working at the law firm where she was employed. She said when asked if she would come back, 'I no longer believe in the law but I believe in justice.' So she went back to work.

Paul too had witnessed many killings in his days as a zealous follower of Jewish law. Perhaps he had even participated in evil himself. When Jesus revealed himself to Paul, He exclaimed 'Paul, why do you persecute me?'

And has not our own experience taught us the brutal nature of life. The strong persecute the weak. The powerful do anything to hold onto power. We ourselves have a hard time not trampling over others when our interests are at stake. In the news right now we have Former Egyptian President Mubarak hiding away at a resort villa. He knows full well that the military establishment from which he came will let him keep the billions he siphoned off the backs of the people. I heard yesterday that Moammar Gadhafi has squired away a cool thirty billion or so. Do you think he is going to give up that power trip without a fight?

And so we are not justified by the law because left to our own accord we can't keep it.

Paul wrote profoundly that 'We know that a person is justified not by works of the law but through faith in Jesus Christ . . . And the life I now live in the flesh I live by faith in the Son of God, who loved me and gave himself for me.' Galatians 2:16. 20

'You foolish Galatians! Who has bewitched you?' The only thing I want to learn from you is this: Did you receive the Spirit by doing the works of the law or by believing what you heard? . . . The one who is righteous will live by faith.' Galatians 3:1, 11

Paul does tend to get a bit testy at times but all for good reason. He says to the Galatians:

'For freedom, Christ has set you free . . . For you were called to freedom, brothers and sisters, only do not use your freedom as an opportunity for self-indulgence, but through love become slaves to one another. For the whole law is summed up in a single commandment, you shall love your neighbor as yourself.' Galatians 5:1,13-15

'Live by the Spirit, I say and do not gratify the desires of the flesh' . . . we know what this means . . . . 'By contrast, the fruit of the Spirit is love, joy, peace, patience, kindness, generosity, faithfulness, gentleness and self-control . . . . If we live by the Spirit, we are also guided by the Spirit.' Galatians 5:16,22-23

'Bear one another's burden's, and this way you will fulfill the law of Christ . . . . May I never boast of anything except the cross of our Lord

Jesus Christ, by which the world has been crucified to me, and I to the world. For neither circumcision or uncircumcision is anything, but a new creation is everything. . . . May the grave of our Lord Jesus Christ be with your spirit, brothers and sisters. Amen.' Galatians 6:2,14,15,18

Ephesians - Next in the Bible, Paul or one of his pupils wrote to the churches in the region of Asia Minor know as Ephesus. 'Bonnie Thurston writes, 'The main theme of Ephesians is God's plan to reconcile Jews and Gentiles, which was accomplished through the death and resurrection of Jesus.' Or as Lewis Donelson wrote in his Westminster Bible Companion commentary, 'God has done wonderful things for us in Jesus Christ, and God must be praised . . . . The church, Jews and Gentiles, the family, and the individual are all placed carefully into God's plan for salvation.'

'Blessed be the God and Father of our Lord Jesus Christ, who has blessed us in Christ with every spiritual blessing in the heavenly places, just as he chose us in Christ before the foundation of the world to be holy and blameless before him in love. Ephesians 1:3-4

Donelson adds: The letter also exhorts the ethical life . . . the author takes us into the details of how Christians love each other . . . . In fact, our capacity for love is one of God's blessings to us. We do not bless God by loving each other; rather, God blesses us by enabling us to love.'

'In Him, we have redemption through his blood, the forgiveness of our trespasses, according to the riches of his grace, that the lavished on us . . . . so that we, who were the first to set our hope on Christ, might live for the praise of his glory.' Ephesians 1:7,12

According to Donelson, 'the divine mystery is revealed in the gospel and this mystery concerns the exaltation of Christ, our redemption in him, and the ethical life that ensues.'

'Your were dead through the trespasses and sins in which you once live, following the course of the world, following the ruler of the power of the air, the spirit that is now at work among those who are disobedient . . . . But God, who is rich in mercy, out of the great love which he loved us, even when we were dead through our trespasses, made us alive together in Christ-by grace you have been saved . . . For by grace, you have been saved through faith, and this is not your own doing; it is a gift of God-not the result of works, so that no one may boast.' Ephesians 2:1-2,4-5,8-9

'So he came and proclaimed peace to you who were far off and peace to those who were near, for through him both of us have access in one Spirit to the Father. Ephesians 2:17-18

Donelson: 'There is another reminder here for us that Jews and Christians are eternally connected. Christians cannot tell their story apart for the story of Israel . . . Whatever the unique status of the church might mean, it does not mean that Christians can boast over Jews.'

'The Gentiles have become fellow heirs, members of the same body, and sharers in the promise in Christ Jesus through the gospel.' Ephesians 3:6

'I pray that, according to the riches of his glory, he may grant that you may be strengthened in you inner being with power through his Spirit, and that Christ may dwell in your hearts through faith, as you are being rooted and grounded in love. I pray that you may have the power to comprehend, with all the saints, what is the breath and length and height and depth, and to know the love of Christ that surpasses knowledge, so that you may be filled with all the fullness of God.' 3:16-19

'I therefore, the prisoner in the Lord, beg you to lead a life worthy of the calling to which you have been called, with all humility and gentleness, with patience, bearing one another in love, making every effort to maintain the unity of the Spirit in the bond of peace . . . There is . . . one God and Father of all, who is above all and through all and in all.' Ephesians 4:1-6

'We must no longer be children; tossed to and fro and blown about by every wind of doctrine . . . we must grow up in every way into him who is the head into Christ.' Ephesians 4:4-15

Donelson: 'Christ-based unity shows itself in love, in putting up with each other . . . Our love, our submission to each other, is not done with bravado or applause, but with humility. There is quietness to Christian love that is necessary to its character.'

'You were taught to put away your former way of life, your old self, corrupt and deluded by its lusts, and to be renewed in the spirit of your minds, and to clothe yourselves with the new self, created according to the likeness of God in true righteousness and holiness.' Ephesians 4:22-24

Donelson: On the one hand, all righteousness must emerge from God's own being. All righteousness is a reflection of God's righteousness. And is one sense God is the ultimate cause of all righteousness and holiness. On the other hand, righteousness involves real humans and real human deeds.'

'So then, putting away falsehood let all of us speak the truth to our neighbors, for we are members of one another. Be angry but do not sin; do not let the sun go down on you anger . . . Let no evil talk come out of your mouths, but only what is useful for building up, as there is need, so that your words may give grace to those who hear . . . and be kind to one another, tenderhearted, forgiving one another as God in Christ has forgiven you . . . . Therefore, be imitators of God, as beloved children, and live in love as Christ loved us and gave himself up for us. Ephesians 4:25-26, 29, 32 and 5:1-2

'Let no one deceive you with empty words . . . entirely outs of place is obscene, silly, and vulgar talk, but instead, let there be thanksgiving . . . . Live as children of light-for the fruit of the light is found in all that is good and right and true. Try and find out what is pleasing to the Lord . . . . Sleeper, awake! Rise from the dead, and Christ will shine on you.' Ephesians 5:4, 9-10, 14

This is lot that could be said of the rest of chapter 5 and part of 6 about the role of men and women in the home. But for me the main idea is set in the first verse. Many twist the rest of the verse around to suit them when it comes to subjecting women to second class status.

'Be subject to one another out of reverence for Christ.' Ephesians 5:1

To me this is the whole of the teaching.

Paul concludes his letter to the Ephesians with a towering message. We Christians are different. Will live differently and we fight differently that the world.

'Finally, be strong in the Lord and in the strength of his power. Put on the whole armor of God, so that you may be able to stand against the wiles of the devil . . . . Stand therefore, and fasten the belt of truth around your waist, and put on the breastplate of righteousness. As shoes for you feet put on whatever will make you ready to proclaim the gospel of peace. With all of these take the shield of faith, with which you will be able to quench all the flaming arrows of the evil one. Take the helmet of salvation, and the sword of the Spirit, which is the word of God.' Ephesians 6:10-11, 13-17

'Grace be with all who have an undying love for our Lord Jesus Christ. Ephesians 6;24

Philippians - As we have discussed earlier it is dangerous to read any of Paul's letters in isolation of one another because we do not always know the questions that he was addressing. In the next book, Paul's treatment of women differs from previous letters. Jouette Bassler writes: 'The founding of the church is described in Acts 16:6-50 but that account provides little help in interpreting the Letter to the Philippians beyond confirming the prominent role of women in the church Phil 4:2-3.'

It seems though the many of the same issues plagued the church in Philippi as the others. That is that they struggled to maintain unity and had a hard time not puffing themselves up. They also were under attack from those that would pervert the Gospel of Christ that they were originally taught.

Paul was actually in jail somewhere when he wrote this letter, suffering for Christ if you will.

'For God is my witness, how I long for all of you with the compassion of Christ Jesus. And this is my prayer, that your love may overflow more and more with knowledge and full insight to help you determine what is best, so that in the day of Christ you may be pure and blameless, having produced the harvest of righteousness that comes though Jesus Christ for the glory and praise of God. Phil 1:8-11

'Only live your life in a manner worthy of the gospel of Christ, so that, whether I come and see you or am absent and hear about you, I will know that you are standing firm in one spirit, striving side by side with one mind for the faith of the gospel, and are in no way intimidated by your opponents . . . For he has graciously granted you the privilege not only of believing in Christ, but of suffering for him as well.' Phil 1:27-28

Barth in his commentary on Philippians says, 'The grace of being permitted to believe in Christ is surpassed by the grace of being permitted to suffer for him, of being permitted to walk the way of Christ with Christ himself to the perfection of fellowship with him. This is where standing fast, being one, and striving for the faith leads: truly not to a Christian triumph but to a Christian defeat . . . To assent to it, is what the 'state' worthy of the gospel ultimately comes to.'

'Do nothing from selfish ambition or conceit, but in humility regard others as better than yourselves. Let each of you look not to your own interests but to the interests of others. Let the same mind be in you that was in Christ Jesus, who, though, he was in the form of God, did not regard equality with God as something to be exploited, but emptied himself, taking the form of a slave, being born in human likeness, and being found in human form, he humbled himself and became obedient to the point of death-even death on a cross.' Phil 2:3-8

Barth: 'He (Paul) takes it for granted that in the face of the 'one thing' there can be room only for humility . . . To believe in grace means, concretely, to set the other above oneself . . . . Which neighbor? The good, clever, earnest, pious one to whom I willingly bow as such? No . . . we are bidden when looking at our neighbor to think of the 'one thing' of grace-to see him, in his foolishness and wickedness it may be, as a messenger of its sovereignty . . . . The confused voice I hear out there, often so unattractive, so contrary to my own subjective outlook, is the voice of the 'one thing'. The disturbance on my island, which every neighbor first of all means for me, is disturbance by the 'one thing' I keep forgetting.'

'Therefore my beloved . . . work out your own salvation with fear and trembling, for it is God who is at work in you, enabling you both to will and to work for his good pleasure. Do all things without murmuring and arguing, so that you may be blameless and innocent, children of God without blemish in the midst of a crooked and perverse generation, in which you shine like stars in the world. Phil 2:12-15

"I press on toward the goal for the prize of the heavenly call of God in Christ Jesus . . . He will transform the body of our humiliation that is may be conformed to the body of his glory. Phil 3:14, 21

Let your gentleness be known to everyone, The Lord is near. Do not worry about anything but in everything by prayer and supplication with thanksgiving let your requests be known to God. And the peace of God, which surpasses all understanding, will guard your hearts and minds in Christ Jesus. Finally, beloved, whatever is true, whatever in honorable whatever is just, whatever is pure, whatever is pleasing, whatever is commendable, if there is any excellence and if there is anything worthy of praise, think about these things. Keep on doing the things that you have learned and received and heard and seen in me, and the God of peace will be with you. Phil 4:5-9

Barth: 'Man is unguarded, open to every enemy and every danger, as long as he does not give thanks, as long as in all the worship and prayer that he perhaps does not neglect, he still keeps his troubles to himself, shut away from God, instead of presenting them to God, revealing them to him as Lord to whom his praises are due.'

Barth: 'But knowing about the Good is knowledge of God only when the Good is a commandment and when the commandment is kept . . . The demand that follows on what we learn and receive from the apostles, hear and see in them can never be anything else but . . . do! . . . The thanksgiving in verse 6 and this doing will not be things to look for far apart.'

'The grace of the Lord Jesus Christ be with your spirit.' Phil 4:23

48th Sunday – Read Colossians, 1 and 2 Thessalonians

'As God's chosen ones, holy and beloved, clothe yourselves with compassion, kindness, humility, meekness, and patience . . . forgive one another . . . Above all clothe yourselves in love.' Col 3:12-14

March 6, 2011

Colossians, 1 Thessalonians, 2 Thessalonians –Each letter in the New Testament puts forth something to help us understand what it means to be a Christian. They share with us issues people were having with faith; the letters encourage and at times correct.

Lewis Donelson, in his Westminster Bible Companion commentary says that in Colossians we learn more about the fundamental Christian ideal of hope. In Colossians the author, 'wants to strengthen the faith of wavering and wandering Christians at Colossae. Through the centuries the letter has reminded Christian readers of the certainty of our salvation, of the power of Christ over all powers, and of the need to love one another . . . the letter takes us from the heart of God, where we learn of God's eternal intentions for creation, to the mundaneness of human relationships.'

Although the letter is gently written, its ideas are profound and can challenge us in our thinking today. How many of us are cozy in our beliefs. We read something and think it sounds good so we buy into that.

There were problems in Colossae during Bible times and there are still big problems in the world today. Evil is rampant. Just look at North Africa where the Gadhafi clan is using airplanes and tanks to hold on to power. Like us, people in Bible times had questions about their faith in the face of danger and uncertainty.

Donelson: Is faith is Jesus sufficient? Do we need outside help against evils of the world?'

We read and talk about Jesus on Sunday morning but Monday through Saturday we trust ourselves and the US military.

The people in Colossae were trying to hedge their bets. Some still wanted to hang on to the polytheistic notions of the past. The author of Colossians needed to remind them of 'the simple Christian ethics of the Christian life: love, submission and forgiveness.'

There aren't any stealth bombers in that.

We are tempted to create our own Christian theology. But the truth of the Gospel message comes from the Bible. It first came from the Apostles who witnessed the risen Christ and who received the power of the Holy Spirit to proclaim the truth about God. That is, who is God, and what are we to do about that. The church in Colossae needed to be reminded of this and so do we.

'To the saints and faithful brothers and sisters in Christ in Colossae: Grace to you and peace from God our Father. In our prayers for you we always thank God, the Father of our Lord Jesus Christ, for we have heard of your faith in Christ Jesus and of the love that you have for all the saints, because of the hope laid up for you in heaven.' Col 1:2-5

Donelson: 'In Colossians, hope is described as the anchor for faith and love . . . Hope, however, manifests itself in love . . . We Christians today in our church debates often separate truth and love. 'I shall hold to the truth of the gospel, and I do not care who gets hurt.' Or 'I shall love you and accept you, not matter what you think or do.' Such exclusive stands have no place here. There is no seam between truth and love. The truth leads to love, and there is not love apart from the truths of the gospel.'

'He is the image of the invisible God, the firstborn of all creation; for in him all things in heaven and on earth were created, things visible and invisible, whether thrones or dominions or rulers or powers—all things have been created through him and for him. He himself is before all things, and in him all things hold together. He is the head of the body, the church; he is the beginning, the firstborn from the dead, so that he might come to have first place in everything. For in him all the fullness of God was pleased to dwell, and through him God was pleased to reconcile to himself all things, whether on earth or in heaven, by making peace through the blood of his cross.' Col 1:15-20

The Colossians had questions and so do we.

Donelson: 'Does the cosmos have benevolent order or not? Is the divine core of the universe accessible to humans or not? Can we live in accordance with God's intentions or not?

'God creates through the divine word or wisdom, and it is word or wisdom that provides order, coherence, and purpose to the world. Furthermore, as proper parts of this creation, human beings possess within themselves this divine word or wisdom. By locating this divine order within themselves and by living according to its prodding, people can live the best life, the life God intended for them.'

And so we might naturally ask at this point, are we 'giving allegiance to powers that are not real powers . . . . The radical commitment to Christian love that Colossians enjoins can be managed only when we understand that Christ is the ultimate power.'

God came down to earth from heaven in the flesh and dwelt among us. Do we believe this is true or not?

To the church at Colossae, 'continue securely established and steadfast in the faith, without shifting from the hope promised in the gospel that you heard.' Col 1:23

Paul proclaims, 'I became its (suffering) servant (the church) according to God's commission that was given to me for you, to make the word of God fully known, the mystery that has been hidden throughout the ages and generations but now has been revealed to his saints . . . . I am saying this so that no one may deceive you with plausible arguments.' Co 1:25, 2:4

Donelson: 1. 'we must have knowledge; 2 the content of this knowledge is Christ himself; 3 this knowledge of Christ gives us hope; 4 this knowledge is inevitability and necessarily accompanied by the life of love.'

'As you therefore, have received Christ Jesus the Lord, continue to live your lives in him, rooted and built up in him an established in the faith, just as you were taught, abounding in thanksgiving . . . . Do not let anyone disqualify you, insisting on self-abasement and worship of angels, dwelling on visions, puffed up without cause by a human way of thinking . . . ' Col 2:6, 18

'So if you have been raised with Christ, seek things that are above where Christ is, seated at the right hand of God . . . As God's chosen ones, holy and beloved, clothe yourselves with compassion, kindness, humility, meekness, and patience . . . forgive each other; just as the Lord has forgiven you . . . Above all clothe yourselves in love . . . And let the peace of Christ rule in your hearts . . . And whatever you do, in word or deed, do everything in the name of the Lord Jesus, giving thanks to God the Father through him.' Col 3:1, 12, 15, 17

Donelson: 'It would be hard to find a better description of the peculiar character of Christian love. Christian love is shaped by personal humility, by vulnerability to the community, by forgiveness.'

'Devote yourselves to prayer, keeping alert in it with thanksgiving . . . Conduct yourselves wisely toward outsiders, making the most of your time . . . I, Paul, write this greeting with my own hand. Remember my chains. Grave be with you.' Col 4:2, 5, 18

Donelson: Colossians raises for me the question of risk. We are called here to risk the Christian life . . . . We must love, submit, follow Christ, even though we cannot think through why such behavior works. We cannot understand love, but we must try to live it.'

1 Thessalonians - is the oldest Christian writing in the New Testament having been written about 20 years after the death and resurrection of Jesus Christ. The earliest converts were a mixture of Jews who already had religion and Gentiles who did not.

Raymond Collins says that Timothy had visited Thessalonica and came back to Paul 'with a generally positive report about the situation, but seems to have hinted at a deficiency in the Thessalonians life of faith. Timothy's report prompted Paul to write this letter.'

Collins goes on to say, 'this letter is the first proclamation of the gospel . . . . It attests to the use of early Christian creedal formulas and the combination of gospel proclamation and moral exhortation. It underscores that the believer's life is one of faith, hope, and love and describes the final salvation as life with Christ . . . . and . . . the affirmation that the resurrection of Jesus is the pledge of his return and the resurrection of believers.'

'Grace to you and Peace . . . for your work of faith, and labor of love and steadfastness of hope in our Lord Jesus Christ. For we know, brothers and sisters beloved by God, that he has chosen you, because our message of the gospel came to you not in word only, but also in power and in the Holy Spirit and with full conviction . . . And you became imitators of us and of the Lord for in spite of persecution you received the word with joy inspired by the Holy Spirit so that you became an example to all the believers in Macedonia and Achaia.' 1 Thes 1:1-7

'Therefore, we sent Timothy . . . to strengthen and encourage you for the sake of your faith . . . because . . . I was afraid that somehow the tempter had tempted you and that our labor had been in vain . . . but Timothy has brought us good news of your faith and love.' 1 Thes 3:1,2,5

'May the Lord make you increase and abound in love for one another and for all . . . And may he so strengthen your hearts in holiness that you may be blameless before our God and Father at the coming of our Lord Jesus with all his saints.' 1 Thes 3:12-13

Paul goes on to describe what is like to live a life that is pleasing to God. 'For this is the will of God, your sanctification . . . . for God did not call us to impurity but in holiness . . . . love one another . . . aspire to live quietly, to mind your own affairs, and to work with your own hands.' 1 Thes 4 3,7,9,11

'For since we believe that Jesus died and rose again even so, through Jesus, God will bring with him those who have died . . . For the Lord himself, with a cry of command, with the archangel's call and with the sound of God's trumper, will descend from heaven, and the dead in Christ will rise first. Then we who are alive, who are left, will be caught up in the clouds together with them to meet the Lord in the air, and so we will be with the Lord forever. Therefore, encourage one another with these words.' 1 Thes 4:14,16-18

The earliest Christians thought Christ would come back before they died. But it was taking longer than they expected so Paul reminded the people that the timing of these things were not for them to know.

'Now concerning the times and seasons . . . . you yourselves know very well that the day of the Lord will come like a thief in the night. When they say, 'There is peace and security, then destruction will come upon them . . . But you beloved, are not in darkness, for that day to surprise you like a thief; for you are all children of the light and children of the way . . . so then let us not fall asleep as others do, but let us keep awake and be sober . . . put on the breastplate of faith and love, and for a helmet the hope of salvation. For God has destined us not for wrath but for obtaining salvation through our Lord Jesus Christ.

We urge you, beloved, to admonish the idlers, encourage the faint heated, help the weak, be patient with all of them . . . . seek to do good . . . rejoice always, pray without ceasing, give thanks in all circumstances, for this is the will of God in Christ Jesus for you.

'May the God of peace himself sanctify you entirely . . . the grace of our Lord Jesus Christ be with you.' 1 Thes 5

2 Thessalonians – follows the same basic outline as the first. The earliest Christians were waiting on Christ to return. When he did not come right away, the teachers had to encourage them to persevere.

'As to the coming of the Lord Jesus Christ and our being gathered to him, we beg you, brothers and sisters, not to be quickly be shaken in mind or alarmed . . . let no one deceive you in any way . . . So then brothers and sisters stand firm and hold fast to the traditions that you were taught by us, either by word of mouth or by our letter.

May the Lord direct your hearts to the love of God and to the steadfastness of Christ . . . . keep away from believers who are living in idleness and not according to the tradition that they received from us. For you yourselves know how you ought to imitate us, we were not idle when we were with you, and we did not eat anyone's bread without paying for it, but with toil and labor we worked night and day, so that we might not burden any of you.

Now may the Lord of peace himself give you peace at all times and in all ways.' 2 Thes 3:16

49th Sunday – Read 1 and 2 Timothy, Titus, Philemon

'Do good, be rich in good works, generous, and ready to share so that we may take hold of the life that really is life.' 1 Tim 6:18-19

This saying is sure; Christ came into the world to save sinners. 1 Tim 1:15

March 13, 2011

1 Timothy, 2 Timothy, Titus and Philemon – When we read the Bible, what are we really learning about? Kalas writes in the 'A Hop, Skip, and a Jump through the Bible,' 'in its entirety, it is God's story. Even when God isn't mentioned, God is still the brooding presence, wonderfully and sometimes fearfully inescapable.' Kalas goes to say that surprisingly with all the different types of literature in the Bible, written over a long period of time by lots people who didn't know each other, there is a plot to the Bible. 'And what is the plot, It is the story of God's relationship with our human race . . . And as the plot unfolds in the pages of scripture we sense that it is at work still in our lives, our times, our circumstances, and our decisions. And the better we understand the scripture plot, the readier we are to contribute to the redemption of our planet through our own participation in the eternal plot.'

As much as we might like to read in the Bible that we are supposed to live for ourselves, get as much fame and wealth as we can, and live happy lives secluded from problems, it is not in there. There is a popular wave of preaching called the prosperity gospel. Prosperity sells because it feels good. It is not however the real gospel. The real gospel calls for our contemplation on the main character of the Bible. That is God. God created the world. We do not know when or how he did this but we know why, because he loves us. He created righteousness, justice and mercy as our calling not so that we might miss out on some fun, but so that we might live fulfilled. But God took a great risk in his creation of us. He did not attach puppet strings to control our every move. God gave us freedom to decide if we would love him back. Our reading thus far indicates that clearly we missed the mark. God might have manifested himself in many ways to draw attention to him. Might he have created a morning sunrise or beautiful mountains and waterfalls to capture our attention? Might he have created a cycle of nature that allows us to sustain ourselves? Might God have given us the ability to reason and love? For some strange reason these things were not enough. Man has fallen short on righteousness. In the mysterious phrase 'in the fullness of time, God came down to earth. Not as a mighty warrior with thunderbolts but born in the flesh by a peasant girl named Mary in a manger no less because there was no room for them at the inn. The boy, who was God, did not dwell on this fact but in every moment of his life on how to do the will of Father. He grew to manhood and preached that we ought to love God with all our heart our strength and our mind and our neighbor as ourselves. He taught that we needed to forgive and that we needed not to be concerned with wealth and power, but that we should strive do to the will God. He said things we didn't want to hear and we hung him on a tree and killed him. But he didn't stay in the tomb. He rose from the dead and gave his closest followers a promise. He said he would send the Holy Spirit to guide them. He told them to stay together and teach people the gospel message.

There is a definite pattern in the New Testament. The message lays out a narrow way to live. As the Good News is proclaimed, people are fascinated at first. But then a little time goes by the people start changing their opinions. They start relying on themselves again and try and change the gospel message they heard. They control and manipulate to get what they want. They develop power struggles and the list goes on and on. We do not have all the details in the Bible of exactly what transpired in each local church that was started. But we do have a few of the cherished letters that were saved.

Kalas: 'These books survived not because some organization endorsed them, but because tens of thousands of ordinary and extraordinary believers read them, loved them, copied them and passed them on.'

As we wind down the reading of the Bible in a year, we get to several books called Pastoral Epistles.

Kalas: The three letters are often identified as the Pastoral Epistles, because they contain so much counsel to the young church leaders.'

In 1 Timothy, we get a little twist to the typical Pauline greeting. Instead of grace and peace, we get grace, mercy, and peace from God the Fathers and Christ Jesus our Lord. The two Timothy letters are the only place we get the 'triad' according to Donelson in his Westminster Bible companion commentary.

As we have come to expect, there are still problems in the early church.

Paul states that he is writing, 'so that you may instruct certain people not to teach any different doctrine and not to occupy themselves with myths and endless genealogies that promote speculation rather than divine training that is known by faith. But the aim of such instruction is love that comes from a pure heart, a good conscience, and sincere faith. Some people have deviated from these and turned to meaningless talk . . . . without understanding either what they are saying or the things about which they make assertions.' 1 Timothy 1:3-7

For us today, we must not be lured in to false thinking by those who would have us believe another gospel than what is written in the Bible. And to know how to discern, we have to know the Bible.

'This saying is sure and worthy of full acceptance, that Christ Jesus came into the world to save sinners . . . ' 1 Timothy 1:13

There are five 'sure sayings' in the Pastoral Epistles. They sound like phrases that would have been repeated among the early followers much like a creed would be in our worship today.

'First of all, then, I urge that supplications, prayers, intercessions, and thanksgivings be made for everyone. . . . For there is one God; there is also one mediator between God and humankind, Christ Jesus, himself human, who gave himself a ransom for all.' 1 Timothy 2:1,5-6

Paul goes on to instruct the leaders of the early churches.

''The saying is sure; whoever aspires to the office of bishop desires a noble task. Now a bishop must be above reproach, married only once, temperate, sensible, respectable, hospitable, an apt teacher, not a drunkard, not violent but gentle, not quarrelsome, and not a lover of money . . . . He must manage his own household well . . . for it someone does not know how to manage his own household, how can he take care of God's church . . . . They must hold fast to the mystery of faith. ' 1 Timothy 3:1-6, 9

Donelson: Officers do not define tradition, rather tradition defines the officers. This is the case for all Christians of all times. We do not define the proper shape of the gospel. It is not as though one can always look at us and see what the true Christian is or what Christ is like. Instead, the gospel creates us into new people. Christ lives in us and shapes us, not into ourselves at our best, but as Christians. We do not define Christ, Christ defines us.'

Paul . . . 'I am writing so that you may know how one ought to behave in the household of God which is the church of the living God, the pillar and bulwark of the truth. Without any doubt, the mystery of our religion is great:

He was revealed in flesh,
Vindicated in spirit,
seen by angels,
proclaimed among the Gentiles,
believed in throughout the world,
taken up in glory. 1 Timothy 3:14-16

Back to the scoundrels for a moment:

'They forbid marriage and demand abstinence from food, which God created to be received with thanksgiving by those who believe and know the truth. For everything created by God is good, and nothing is to be rejected, provided it is received with thanksgiving, for it is sanctified by God's word and by prayer.' 1 Timothy 4:3-5

There were groups of people in the first and second generation of the church who were known as Gnostics.

Donelson: 'Gnostics believed that only people with special spiritual knowledge could escape the burdens of the material world and be saved.'

Anyone claiming to have 'special knowledge' is one to be watched out for. We remember that the first Christians did not have New Testaments to carry around and remind them of the gospel message. They had only the oral traditions and then the letters. When they compared the oral traditions with how some were acting, and weighed those against what was recorded in the letters, they decided to save the letters.

'Have nothing to do with profane myths and old wives tales. Train yourselves in Godliness, for while physical training is of some value, godliness is valuable in every way, holding promise for both the present life and the life to come. The saying is sure and worthy of full acceptance. For this end we toil and struggle, because we have our hope set on the living God, who is the Savior of all people, especially those who believe . . . . set the believers an example in speech and conduct, in love, faith, in purity. 1 Timothy 4:7-12

Paul gives a list of things that the Christian should avoid; including the love of money which he says is 'a root of all kinds of evil.'

'But as for you, man of God, shun all this; pursue righteousness, godliness, faith, love, endurance, gentleness. Fight the good fight of the faith; take hold of the eternal life, to which you were called and for which you made the good confession . . . do good, be rich in good works, generous, and ready to share . . . . so that they may take hold of the life that really is life.' 1 Timothy 6:10-13, 18-19

2 Timothy – Like the first, the second letter written by Paul to Timothy was meant to be read by other churches that Paul established. Its purpose was to teach correct doctrine.

Donelson: 'The most notable absence is the reduced concern for church offices. This letter will focus on the themes of suffering and death to an extent not anticipated in 1 Timothy.'

'I am reminded of your sincere faith, a faith that lived first in your grandmother Lois and your mother Eunice and now, I am sure, lives in you . . . . Do not be ashamed then, of the testimony about our Lord or of me his prisoner, but join with me in suffering for the gospel, relying on the power of God, who saved us and called us with a holy calling, not according to our works but according to his own purpose and grace . . . . Hold to the standard of sound teaching that you have heard from me, in the faith and love that are in Christ Jesus. Guard the good treasure entrusted to you, with the help of the Holy Spirit living in us.' 2 Timothy 1:5, 8-9, 13-14

Donelson: 'Herein lies the first aspect of the problem of suffering that will dominate this letter. The story of Jesus is an embarrassment. To have the Lord of the church be crucified, to have the eternal judge of heaven and earth die on a cross, is a scandal . . . . Paul is asking Timothy, and through Timothy, all church leaders, to take on the suffering that comes with the gospel. This suffering can be endured only through the empowerment of the Spirit and through the promise of reward.'

'Share in the suffering like a good solider of Christ Jesus . . . Remember Jesus Christ, raised from the dead, a descendent of David-that is my gospel, for which I suffer hardship, even to the point of being chained like a criminal. But the word of God is not chained . . . This saying is sure:

If we have died with him, we will also live with him;
If we endure, we will also reign with him;
If we deny him, he will also deny us;
If we are faithless, he remains faithful;
For he cannot deny himself. 2 Timothy 2:3,8-13

'Shun youthful passions and pursue righteousness, faith, love, and peace along with those who call on the Lord from a pure heart . . . And the Lord's servant must not be quarrelsome but kindly to everyone, an apt teacher, patient, correcting opponents with gentleness.' 2 Timothy 2:22-25

'For people will be lovers of themselves, lovers of money, boasters, arrogant, abusive, disobedient to their parents, ungrateful, unholy, inhumane, implacable, slanderers, profligates, brutes, haters of good, treacherous, reckless with swollen conceit, lovers of pleasure, rather than lovers of God, holding to the outward form of godliness but denying its power. Avoid them! 2 Timothy 3:2-5

'Now you have observed my teaching, my conduct, my aim in life, my faith, my patience, my love, my steadfastness, my persecutions and suffering . . . Indeed all who want to live a godly life in Christ Jesus will be persecuted . . . . I solemnly urge you: proclaim the message, be persistent whether the time is favorable or unfavorable; convince rebuke, and encourage, with the utmost patience in teaching.' 2 Timothy 3:10-11,4:1-2

Donelson: 'Old sins should not be confused with good tradition. Thus the debate that animates the Pastoral Epistles has not gone away. What is sound tradition, and what is not?'

'The Lord be with your spirit. Grace be with you.' 2 Timothy 4:22

Donelson: 'To be a Christian is not simply to be more of what we already are; to be a Christian is to die and be reborn . . . . The reality of the cross, of death, of suffering connected with death cannot be fathomed. The cross cannot produce tame propositions in our theology.'

Titus – is the shortest of the three Pastoral Letters written to be shared with a relatively young church in Crete. According to Abraham Smith, repeatedly, this letter emphasizes a concern for the unsaved and see the good work of believers as a part of God's redemptive plan for the entire world.' Like the other letters it does express concern over teaching the 'right' gospel.

'They profess to know God, but they deny him by their actions.' Titus 1:16

'But as for you, teach what is consistent with sound doctrine . . . Show yourself in all respects a model of good works, and in your teaching show integrity, gravity, and sound speech that cannot be censured . . . . For the grace of God has appeared, bringing salvation to all, training us to renounce impiety and worldly passions, and in the present age to live lives that are self controlled, upright, and godly, while we wait for the blessed hope and manifestation of the glory of our great God and Savior, Jesus Christ.' Titus 2:1,7-8,11-13

Donelson: 'The marvels of God's deeds in Jesus Christ come to life in the mundane details of our lives. The Christian truths must be lived out in the messiness and confusions of our relationships to each other, both in the house and the church.'

Paul reminds the church once again that we were all once foolish before following Christ.

'But when the goodness and loving kindness of God our Savior appeared, he saved us, not because of any works of righteousness that we had done, but according to his mercy, through the water of rebirth and renewal by the Holy Spirit. This Spirit poured out on us richly through Jesus Christ our Savior, so that, having been justified by his grace; we might become heirs according to the hope of eternal life. The saying is sure.' Titus 3:4-8

Charles Spurgeon in his 'Mornings and Evenings' devotional writes, ' We shall die soon, and then our hope comes from him. Don't we hope that, when we lie upon our sickbed, he will send angels to carry us to His bosom? We believe that when the pulse is faint, and the heart heaves heavily, some angelic messenger shall stand and look with loving eyes upon us, and whisper, Kindred spirit, come away!'

'Grace be with all of you.' Titus 3:15

In summarizing Titus and what well may be the Christian call to a quite moral life, Donelson writes, 'being honest, hardworking, temperate, chaste, and so forth may be admirable, but such quite virtues are probably irrelevant to the major tasks of life, which involves accomplishing something out there. You and I would rarely summarize the Christian life as the pursuit of virtue . . . . When I think of the bitter battles troubling the church and of the vicious and vitriolic tone of the debate; I know that the quite virtues of the Pastoral Epistles would be a blessing to us. Perhaps we can never know who is right or wrong about many social issues, but we can know honesty, gentleness, and modesty. We can treat each other well.'

Philemon – is a strange book, one that I wouldn't quote on my own or comment on without some help.

Kalas: 'At the very least, Philemon is a prime example of how to write a gracious letter.'

Paul writes to Philemon about Onesimus who is either Philemon's brother or his former slave. People have debated the true meaning of this relationship depending on the position they supported. I prefer the former.

Philemon and his brother Onesimus have had a falling out over what looks like money. Paul wants the two to reunite. Paul is willing to pay the debt if that will make reconciliation possible.

'For this reason, though I am bold enough in Christ to command you to do your duty, yet I would rather appeal to you on the basis of love . . . . if he has wronged you in any way or owes you anything, charge that to my account.' Philemon 1:8:18

Allen Callahan thinks that Paul 'insists that the love between those in the Lord cannot be fulfilled when love has grown cold . . . without justice there is not peace, and without peace between the brethren there can be no ministry.'

This is about as much as I can squeeze out of Philemon. Amen.

50th Sunday – Read Hebrews and James

'Let us therefore approach the throne of grace with boldness, so that we may receive mercy and find grace for help in time of need.' Heb 4:16

March 20, 2011

Hebrews and James – O boy! We get toward the end of the New Testament and think the reading will be a breeze. Finding the reading a little heavy, some churchgoers and preachers skip over Hebrews. According to Frances

Taylor Gench in his Westminster Bible Companion commentary this is because of 'its densely woven argument is complex and sustained, and its imagery of priesthood and sacrificial ritual emerges from an ancient world of thought this is quite foreign to our own.'

But as Gench suggests if we stick with Hebrews we will be rewarded because the 'ancient situation, turns out to be strikingly contemporary in its relevance to our situation today. In sum, Hebrews addressed believers who have grown weary in the Christian way and who are in danger of abandoning their Christian vocation.'

As we look over Hebrews it is the only text in the New Testament that points to Jesus in the image of a priest. This brings to mind the ancient Israelite tribe of the Levites who had control over temple matters and basically intervened to God on behalf of the people. The first Christians were Jewish and many still needed theological help in making the full transition. Therefore, the author of Hebrews gives them ideas of Jesus' significance in terms that they can relate to. That is Christ as the sole mediator before God.

Another thought the Gench asks us to consider before reading Hebrews is that the author shows in his argument how Christianity is superior to Judaism. This letter has been used by some to degrade our fellow Jewish sojourners of faith.

Gench: 'Hebrews does not simply celebrate the superiority of Christianity; it also denigrates ancient Israelite religion and practices, declaring them ineffectual.'

But we should keep in mind that the audience to whom the author was writing was Jewish-Christians who may have been tempted to go back to being just Jews. Since this time, Jews and Christians have long parted ways. 'Contemporary Christians must therefore exercise sensitivity and caution in their interpretation and appropriation of Hebrews.'

There is more than one voice that speaks to this issue in the New Testament. God is God of and for all. We could not understand the New Testament if we didn't have the Old. God in my view still has a special place for his Jewish faithful as indicated by the fact that this small group of people is still around after 4,000 years.

Finally, Gench reminds us that Hebrews reads more like a sermon that a letter that we have been used to reading since leaving the Gospels.

'Long ago God spoke to our ancestors in many and various ways by the prophets, but in these last days he has spoken to us by a Son . . . He is the reflection of God's glory and the exact imprint of God's very being, and he sustains all things by his powerful word.' Hebrews 1:1-3

Gench: What this means is that we live in a new age. The decisive events in God's plan for the world-crucifixion and exaltation of Jesus have taken place, and God's purposes for the world now move towards its completion.'

We also get stunning language in the description of who Christ really is as a 'reflection of God's glory and exact imprint of God.'

'Therefore, we must pay greater attention to what we have heard, so that we do not drift away from it . . . . how can we escape if we neglect so great a salvation!' Hebrews 2:1, 3

Gench says that Hebrews does as good a job as any document in the New Testament showing the divinity and humanity of Christ.

'It was fitting that God, for whom and through whom all things exist in bringing many children to glory, should make the pioneer of their salvation perfect through sufferings.' Therefore, he had to become like his brothers and sisters in every respect, so that he might be a merciful and faithful high priest in the service of God, to make a sacrifice of atonement for the sins of the people. Because he himself was tested by what he suffered, he is able to help those who are being tested.' Hebrews 2:10, 17-18

'Christ, however, was faithful over God's house as a son, and we are his house if we hold firm the confidence and the pride that belong to hope.' Hebrews 3:6

'Today, if you hear his voice, do not harden your hearts.' Hebrews 3:7,15, 4:7

Gench: With the repetition of the word 'today', Hebrews underlines the fact that every day of our lives presents opportunities for faithfulness, for responding in obedience to the promises of God . . . . May Hebrews vision of the great salvation that God has made available in Christ rekindle in all of us faithful and responsive hearts!'

'Let us therefore approach the throne of grace with boldness, so that we may receive mercy and find grace to help in time of need.' Hebrews 4:16

'In the days of his flesh, Jesus offered up prayers and supplications, with loud cries and tears, to the one who was able to save him from death, and he was heard because of his reverent submission . . . he learned obedience through what he suffered and having been made perfect, he became the source of eternal salvation for all who obey him.' Hebrews 5:7-9

'About this we have much to say that is hard to explain, since you have become dull in understanding. For though by this time you ought to be teachers, you need someone to teach you again the basic elements of the oracles of God.' Hebrews 5:11-12

Gench reminds us that the one unforgivable sin is one of apostasy. That is 'having tasted the goodness of the word of God and powers of the age to come, and then fallen away, since on their own they are crucifying again the son of God and are holding him up to contempt.' Hebrews 6:5-6

Modern Christians need to hear this too. We have to be active in our faith.

Gench says how here:
-Carefully study the scriptures
-Listen to the great cloud of witnesses
-Join together in worship, study, service, and fellowship
-Stretch our minds with programs of reading and Christian education
-Reflect together on issues that face us in the world in seeking to embody God's purposes for human life.

'We want each one of you to show the same diligence so as to realize the full assurance of hope . . . We have this hope, a sure and steadfast anchor of the soul, a hope that enters inner shrine behind the curtain.' Hebrews 6:11,19

Hebrews goes on in chapter 7 and 8 to make an elaborate argument that Jesus is the true high priest that sacrificed for us. Therefore, we do not need to old Levitical priests to do this for us any longer. The prophets of old predicted that a new covenant would come and it did.

'The days are surely coming, says the Lord, When I will establish a new covenant with the house of Israel and with the house of Judah . . . For I will be merciful toward their iniquities, and I will remember their sins no more . . . . He is the mediator of the new covenant.' Hebrews 8:8,12,15

"Now faith is the assurance of things hoped for, the conviction of things not seen. Indeed, by faith our ancestors received approval. By faith we understand that the worlds were prepared by the word of God, so that what is seen was made from things that are not visible. Hebrews 11:1-3

An epic list is given of the past faithful. And then we are reminded.

'All of these died in faith without having received their promises, but from a distance they saw and greeted them.' Hebrews 11:13

'Therefore, since we are surrounded by so great a cloud of witnesses, let us also lay aside every weight and the sin that clings so closely, and let us run with perseverance the race that is set before us, looking to Jesus the pioneer and perfecter of our faith.' Hebrews 12:1-2

Gench: Faith, however, sustains believers in the face of the world's hostility. It enables them to persevere in the midst of suffering.'

'Consider him who endured such hostility against himself from sinners, so that you may not grow weary of lost heart. In your struggle against sin you have not yet resisted to the point of shedding your blood . . . . Therefore, lift your drooping hands and strengthen your weak knees, and make straight paths for your feet, so that what is lame may not be put out of joint, but rather be healed.' Hebrews 12:3,12

Gench: Hebrews call us to look to Jesus, to follow him as a model, and to trust that suffering in discipleship to Jesus shapes us in his pattern and makes us stronger in faith and witness.'

'Pursue peace with everyone, and the holiness without which no one will see the Lord . . . . let us give thanks, by which we offer to God and acceptable worship with reverence and awe. Hebrews 12:14, 28

'Let mutual love continue. Do not neglect to show hospitality to strangers, for by doing that some have entertained angels with knowing it . . . Do not neglect to do good and to share what you have, for such sacrifices are pleasing to God . . . . Pray for us.' Hebrews 13:1-2,16, 18

James – We remember James from the Jerusalem council who ruled that Gentiles did not have to follow Jewish law. Is this Jesus' brother who wrote this letter? Church tradition says this is so. In any case, we do know that this James according to Gench 'was a dedicated advocate of the Jewish-Christian piety who attached great importance to observance of the Jewish law . . . . The author is an early Christian teacher, one who is responsible for guiding early Christian communities in many aspects of its life.'

The book is not without critics. Martin Luther called James an 'epistle of straw.'

Gench: 'The reasons are readily apparent. Upon the first reading of the letter, one is struck by the glaring absence of central tenets of Christian faith.'

That is because there is not much in James directly about Jesus' 'life, ministry, death or resurrection.'

Also the book of James is famous for it depiction of 'works.' This is in contrast to Paul's teaching that we are justified by faith through grace and not works.

Gench points out that James knew the story of Jesus and his followers knew this too.

Gench: This insight is crucial for one's reading and interpretation of this letter, for the purpose of the letter becomes clear: James is not trying to evangelize the world; instead, it is calling its readers to live the Christian life. The letter of James is not a missionary document; it is an in-house document, a document for use within the church . . . . This is the focus of James. James urges believers to apply Christian faith to every aspect of life.'

Gench: Biblical scholar Luke T. Johnson maintains that the theological lynch-pin of this letter is found in James 3:13-4:10, where James squarely sets two alternatives before us and asks us to choose between friendship with the world or friendship with God.'

'So which will it be? Will we share the attitudes and values and perceptions of the world and live as though God has no claim on our lives? Or will we embrace the attitude and values and perceptions of God and live in a manner that acknowledges God's claim on our lives?

'James, a servant of God and of the Lord Jesus Christ, to the twelve tribes in the Dispersion: Greetings.' James 1:1

'If any of you is lacking is wisdom, ask God, who gives to all generously and ungrudgingly, and it will be given to you. But ask in faith, never doubting, for the one who doubts is like a wave of the sea, driven and tossed by the wind, for the doubter, being double-minded and unstable in every way, must not expect to receive anything from the Lord.' James 1:5-8

Gench: the doubters' indecisiveness, or 'double-mindedness,'; stands in contrast to the wholeness and integrity that is James' hope for Christian life.'

'Every generous act of giving, with every perfect gift, is from above, coming down from the Father of lights, with whom there is no variation or shadow due to change. In fulfillment of his own purpose he gave us birth by the word of truth, so that we would become a kind of first fruits of his creatures.' James 1:17-18

'You must understand this, my beloved: be quick to listen, slow to speak, slow to anger, for your anger does not produce God's righteousness . . . . and welcome with meekness the implanted word that has the power to save your souls' James 1:19-21

Gench: 'They must listen carefully and patiently to God before they presume to speak and act in God's name.'

'But be doers of the word, and not merely hearers who deceive themselves.' James 1:22

'If they think they are religious, and do not bridle their tongues but deceive their hearts, their religion is worthless. Religion that is pure and undefiled before God, the Father, is this: to care for orphans and widows in their distress, and to keep oneself unstained by the world.' James 1:26-37

Gench: Religion then is a great deal more than doctrine or rituals . . . the test of genuine religion is not orthodoxy (right belief) but orthopraxy (right practice).'

James steps on our toes when he says we would rather hob-nob with the rich and famous than help those who are down on their luck.

My brothers and sisters, do you with your acts of favoritism really believe in our glorious Lord Jesus Christ? . . . 'Has not God chosen the poor in the world to be rich in faith and to be heirs of the kingdom that he has promised to those who love him? . . . You do well if you really fulfill the royal law according to the scripture, 'you shall love your neighbor as yourself . . . . So speak and act as those who are to be judged by the law of liberty . . . . mercy triumphs over judgment.' James 2:5,8, 12-13

Gench: 'The author insists that partiality toward the rich is also a transgression of the biblical principle of love.'

'What good is it, my brothers and sisters, if you say you have faith, but do not have any works? . . . If a brother or sister is naked and lacks daily food, and one of you says to them, 'Go in peace; keep warm and eat your fill.' And yet you do not supply their bodily needs, what is the good of that? . . . For just as the body without the spirit is dead, so faith without works is also dead.' James 2:14-16, 26

Gench: James is best known for its insistence on the inseparable connection between faith and works.'

In the closing chapters James admonishes us to watch our mouth. He also contrasts worldly wisdom with Godly wisdom.

'How great a forest is set ablaze by a small fire! And the tongue is the fire.' James 3:5

'But the wisdom from above is pure, then peaceable, gentle, willing to yield, full of mercy and good fruits, without a trace of partiality or hypocrisy.

And the harvest of righteousness is sown in peace for those who make peace.' James 3:17-18

'Do you not know that friendship with the world is enmity with God? God yearns jealously for the spirit that he has made to dwell in us . . . God opposes the proud, but gives grace to the humble.' James 4:4,5-6

'Submit yourselves therefore to God . . . Draw near to God, and he will draw near to you . . . Humble yourselves before the Lord, and he will exalt you.' James 4:7-8, 10

James concludes with an exhortation about seeking material wealth and about having a prayerful Christian life.

'What is your life? For you are a mist that appears for a little while and then vanishes. Instead you ought to say, 'If the Lord wishes, we will do this or that.' James 4:14-15

'Be patient, therefore, beloved, until the coming of the Lord . . . Indeed we call blessed those who showed endurance . . . . Confess your sins to one another, and pray for one another, so that you may be healed. The prayer of the righteous is powerful and effective.' James 5:7, 11, 16

51st Sunday – Read 1 and 2 Peter, 1,2,3 John, Jude

'God is love, and those who abide in love abide in God, and God abides in them.' 1 John 4:16

'Children, let us love, not in speech, but in truth and action.' 1 John 3:18

March 27, 2011

1 Peter, 2 Peter, 1 John, 2 John, 3 John, Jude – This week we have two decent size epistles and four small ones. I read Fred Craddock's Westminster Bible Companion commentary on the Peter's and Jude and will reference some of his thoughts.

While we may not have all our questions answered about who, what, when and where when we read New Testament letters, 'the recipients of these letters very likely understood every word they heard (letters were read aloud in the churches) because this mail was to them and about them,' according to Craddock.

Craddock: One thing we wish to know is, who is Jesus Christ portrayed in this letter? This is not primarily a historical question; we are continually faced with the question, who is Jesus Christ for us today? And 1 Peter lies among the authoritative sources from which we seek answers . . . All of this to ask, what was it to be Christian in the time and place those of first readers? The extent to which we can know that will be the extent to which we can listen to the letter for ourselves.'

1 Peter, like other New Testament letters was written to encourage and correct. In addition some letters like Peter were written to communities who were undergoing suffering, either in the form of persecution or alienation from the community at large.

Craddock: Tension is there, to be sure, between believers and their culture. Repeatedly the readers are reminded that they are pilgrims, exiles, aliens in the world, but in the household of God they have a new family, a new home. Even so, how does this new family relate to governing authorities and social institutions with which they must deal every day? And how does the church respond to a society that is making life miserable for Christians.'

'Peter, an apostle of Jesus Christ, To the exiles of Dispersion . . . who have been chosen and destined by God the Father and sanctified by the Spirit to be obedient to Jesus Christ . . . . May grace and peace be yours in abundance.' 1 Peter 1;1-2

Craddock: 'And it is not coincidental that the two words of greeting join two heritages" 'grace' from the Gentile culture, 'peace' from the Jewish.'

'Blessed be God . . . by his great mercy he has given us new birth . . . through the resurrection of Jesus Christ from the dead, and into an inheritance that is imperishable, undefiled, and unfading, kept in heaven for you . . . . In this you rejoice, even if now for a little while you have had to suffer various trials . . . Although you have not seen him, you love him; and even though you do not see him now, you believe in him and rejoice with an indescribable and glorious joy, for you are receiving the outcome of your faith, the salvation of your souls . . . . things into which angels long to look' 1 Peter 1:3-4,8-9

Craddock: All teaching and preaching properly begin and end in praise of God.'

'Therefore, prepare your minds for action . . . Do not be conformed to the desires that you formerly had in ignorance. Instead, as he who called you is holy, be holy yourselves in all your conduct.' 1 Peter 1:13-15

Craddock: 'In religious literature of the day, persons too enamored with the immediate pleasures of life were said to be drunk, asleep, and ignorant of higher values. Hence, the New Testament's frequent call for sobriety, being awake, and turning from a life of ignorance . . . . How has God behaved toward us? This is what it means to be holy in all our relationships.'

'Beloved, I urge you as aliens and exiles to abstain from the desires of the flesh that wage war against the soul . . . . For the Lord's sake accept the authority of every human institution, whether of the emperor as supreme, or of governors, as sent by him to punish those who do wrong and to praise those who do right. Honor everyone. Love the family of believers. Fear God. Honor the emperor.' 1 Peter 2:11, 13-14. 17

Craddock: 'This includes the Roman Empire under which the churches addressed in 1 Peter lived.'

Not all Christians in all times were being burned at the stake. There was a time in which Christians were just considered odd people. These folks needed to be reminded that they needed to get along with their communities.

There is more talk in chapter 2 and 3 of slaves and about women taking second fiddle in the household. I will skip over that since I have commented on it before.

'Finally, all of you have unity of spirit, sympathy, love for one another, a tender heart, and a humble mind. Do not repay evil for evil or abuse for abuse, but, on the contrary, repay with a blessing. 1 Peter 3:8-9

Craddock: Verse 8 describes life as it should be within the fellowship: mutual love, singlemindedness, sympathy, tenderness, and humility.'

'Always be ready to make your defense to anyone who demands from you an accounting for the hope that is in you; yet do it with gentleness and reverence . . . . live the rest of your earthly life no longer by human desires but by the will of God.' 1 Peter 3:15, 4:2

'And most of all clothe yourself with humility in your dealings with one another, for 'God opposes the proud, but gives grace to the humble . . . . Cast all your anxiety on him, because he cares for you. Discipline yourselves, keep alert. Like a roaring lion your adversary the devil prowls around, looking for someone to devour. Resist him, steadfast in your faith, for you know that your brothers and sisters in all the world are undergoing the same kinds of suffering. And after you have suffered for a little while, the God of grace . . . will himself restore, support, strengthen, and establish you. To him be the power forever and ever. Amen. 1 Peter 5:5, 7-11

2 Peter – Peter's ire is up at the folks causing problems to some church community in Asia Minor.

Craddock: '2 Peter engages in quite a bit of name calling. Granted, the writer is vigorously involved in a battle with certain persons in the church who are regarded as both wrong and dangerous to the community of faith . . . The primary purpose of the letter is to warn the church, to counter the false prophets, and to rehabilitate the teaching concerning the coming of the day of the Lord.'

'To those who have received a faith as precious as ours through the righteousness of our God and Savior Jesus Christ . . . . His divine power has given us everything needed for life and godliness through the knowledge of him who called us by his own glory and goodness.' 2 Peter 1:1, 3

'For this very reason, you must make every effort to support your faith with goodness, and goodness with knowledge, and knowledge with self-control, and self-control with endurance, and endurance with godliness, and godliness with mutual affection, and mutual affection with love . . . . For in this way, entry into the eternal kingdom of our Lord and Savior Jesus Christ will be richly provided for you.' 2 Peter 1:5-7

Craddock: 'The message seems to be: If you will make provision for your faith with the following virtues (v. 5), God will make provision for your entry into the eternal kingdom.'

Who wants in?

'Therefore, I intend to keep on reminding you on these things, though you know them already and are established in the truth that has come you.' 2 Peter 1:12

'But false teachers also arose among the people, just as there will be false teachers among you, who will secretly bring in destructive opinions. They will deny the Master who brought them . . . ' 2 Peter 2:1

'These people, however are like irrational animals, mere creatures of instinct, born to be caught and killed . . . . These are waterless springs and mists driven by a storm; for whom the deepest darkness has been reserved . . . They promise freedom, but they themselves are slaves to corruption; for people are slaves to whatever masters them. 2 Peter 2:12, 19

'For it would have been better for them never to have known the way of righteousness than, after knowing it, to turn back from the holy commandment that was passed to them. It has happened to them according to the true proverb,

'The dog turns back to its own vomit.'

'The sow is washed only to wallow in the mud.' 2 Peter 2:21-22

Craddock: 'The stern and harsh conclusion to chapter 2 is unsurpassed in the New Testament, but not without its companion texts. Jesus spoke of some acts so contradictory to God's will that it would have been better if the perpetrator had been dropped into the sea with a millstone tied to the neck . . . or even never been born at all.'

'First of all you must understand this, that in the last days scoffers will come, scoffing and indulging their own lusts and saying 'Where is the promise of his coming? . . . But do not ignore this one fact, that with the Lord one day is like a thousand years, and a thousand years are like one day. The Lord is not slow about his promise, as some think of slowness, but is patient with you, not wanting any to perish, but all to come to repentance. But the day of the Lord will come like a thief, and then the heavens will pass away . . . ' 2 Peter 3:3-4, 8-10

Craddock: 'It is evident, however, that with the adversaries the doctrine of the Lord's return is but a specific element in a larger pattern of cynical skepticism . . . Faith that does not believe in the providence and in the final triumph of God experiences disappointment and delay.'

' . . . What sort of persons ought you to be in leading lives of holiness and godliness, waiting for and hastening the coming of the day of God . . . while you are waiting for these things, strive to be found by him at peace, without spot or blemish . . . grow in the grace and knowledge of our Lord and Savior Jesus Christ. To him be the glory both now and to the day of eternity.' 2 Peter 3:11, 12, 14, 18

Craddock: 'let this letter provide the occasion for coming clear to ourselves what we believe on the subject. It is easy enough to be reactive in one's beliefs: I do not believe in evangelism because of the fraud of televangelists. I do not believe in charitable endeavors because some recipients are ne'er-do-wells. I do not believe in the hereafter because some preachers try and scare their listeners. Having said that, what do I believe? What is my vision of the end of history? To what goal or purpose does life move?'

The three Johns – with the help of Robert Kysar. Kysar says there is some similarity in the wording of these letters to the Gospel of John . . . He cites the use of light and darkness, eternal life and the term abiding as examples.

Kysar: 'The major themes of 1 John include Christ's fleshly incarnation and his saving work; God's love and love among the members of the Christian community ; the nature of Christian morality and the Christians relationship with sin; and the imminence of the end times, or 'last days."

'This is the message we have heard from him and proclaim to you, that God is light and in him there is no darkness at all . . . . If we say that we have no sin, we deceive ourselves and the truth is not is us. If we confess our sins, he who is faithful and just will forgive us our sins and cleanse us from all unrighteousness. If we say that we have not sinned, we make him a liar, and his word in not in us . . . . He is the atoning sacrifice for our sins, not for ours only but also for the sins of the whole world. 1 John 1:5, 8-10, 2:2

'See what love the Father has given us that we should be called children of God; and that is what we are.' 1 John 3:1

'God was revealed for this purpose, to destroy the works of the devil.' 1 John 3:8

'For this is the message you have heard from the beginning, that we should love one another . . . . How does God's love abide in anyone who has the world's goods and sees a brother or sister in need and yet refuses to help? . . . Little children, let us love, not in word or speech but in truth and action.' 1 John 3:11, 17-18

'God is love, and those who abide in love abide in God, and God abides in them . . . .

We know because he first loved us.' 1 John 4:16, 19

'I write these things to you who believe in the name of the Son of God; so that you may know you have eternal life . . . . He is the true God and eternal life. 1 John 5:13, 20

2 John rebuts more scoundrels. It's real short but with a big point: Christ did indeed come in the flesh.

Kysar: 2 John is important theologically because of its view of proper doctrine, which suggests that 'orthodoxy' had emerged as a standard by which to measure the authenticity of all who claim to be Christian

'Many deceivers have gone out into the world, those who do not confess that Jesus Christ has come in the flesh; any such person is the deceiver and the antichrist . . . Do not receive into the house or welcome anyone who comes to you and does not bring this teaching.' 2 John 7, 10

3 John – More dividers.

Kysar: 'Diotrephes is dividing the congregation and defying its authority.'

'Beloved, I pray that all may go well with you and that you may be in good health, just as it is well with your soul . . . . I have no greater joy than this, to hear that my children are walking in the truth. 3 John 2, 4

'But Diotrephes, who likes to put himself first, does not acknowledge our authority. 3 John 9

'Beloved, do not imitate evil but imitate what is good. Whoever does good is from God; whoever does evil has not seen God.' 3 John 11

Peace out.

Jude – This is another small letter that many tend to skip over including preachers. Craddock notes that there isn't a verse from Jude in the Revised Common Lectionary. It is also a lot like the Peter letters in terms of wording.

Craddock: 'We accept as the purpose of this letter what the content rather clearly reveals: that is, to alert the church to the intruders among them who pervert the faith and divide the faithful, and to exhort the believers to stand firm in faith, to grow in grace, and to be renewed in the mercy that Christ shows toward them and that they are to exhibit toward those who falter and fail.'

Whew! That was almost longer than Jude.

'Beloved, while eagerly preparing to write to you about the salvation we share, I find it necessary to write and appeal to you to contend for the faith that was once for all entrusted to the saints. For certain intruders have stolen in among you, people who long ago were designated for this condemnation as ungodly, who pervert the grace of our God into licentiousness and deny our only Master and Lord, Jesus Christ.' Jude 3, 4

Craddock: 'What is at stake is the central body of beliefs, the tradition.'

'These are grumblers and malcontents; they indulge their own lusts; they are bombastic in speech, flattering people to their own advantage . . . . It is these worldly people, devoid of the Spirit, who are causing division. 16, 19

Craddock" Then what might they appear to be? Perhaps articulating leaders with charismatic personalities, preaching and teaching and modeling a new freedom of speech and relationship, and bringing a party spirit to the solemn assembly.'

'But you, beloved, build yourselves up on your most holy faith; pray in the Holy Spirit, keep yourselves in the love of God; look forward to the mercy of our Lord Jesus Christ that leads to eternal life. And have mercy on some who are wavering, save others by snatching them out of the fire.' 20-22

Craddock: 'Everyone is welcome, of course, but not everything goes. Standards are to be observed, and flagrant violations cannot be winked at. On the other hand, some effort at forgiveness and restoration must be made.'

'Now to him who is able to keep you from falling, and to make you stand without blemish in the presence of his glory with rejoicing, to the only God our Savior, through Jesus Christ our Lord, be glory, majesty, power, and authority, before all time and now and forever. Amen.' 24-25

Amen. Come, Lord Jesus!

52nd Sunday – Read Revelation

'Holy, holy, holy, Lord God Almighty, who was, is and is to come.' Rev 4:8

April 3, 2011

Revelation – Apocalyptic literature is in the Bible, but that is not all there is. For some, Bible reading is all about end times and signs of the end. Tune the AM radio dial for a minute and you will likely find some preacher shouting out verses from the book of Revelation. Be fearful. Be ready. The world is about to end. He will point to news about wars and tsunamis. He will know the modern mark of the beast. Conspiracy abounds; first it's a new world currency then it is a proposed superhighway from Mexico to Canada. He knows the real antichrist, first Gorbachev then Bin Laden. There have been plenty of end time predictors since Christ; none have been correct. So what are we to make of the book?

According to the Baker Commentary on the Bible, 'Apocalyptic is visionary, highly symbolic . . . written to comfort, encourage, strengthen, quiet doubts, and show God to be the ultimate victor over evil . . . The book of Revelation touches upon most aspects of early Christian thought . . . John makes reference to God, Christ, the work of Christ, the Holy Spirit, the second coming, the final judgment, heaven, hell, angels, creation, mankind, sin, Satan, demons, history, prayer, worship, Christian living, the church, prophesy, the Bible, perseverance, saints, and the profound mystery of God's eternity and its relation to time.'

What we might say about the whole Bible, we can say here too.

Baker Commentary: 'Central to the book is the existence, power, sovereignty, justice, wisdom, and goodness of God. God is . . . . He is the almighty and he is in control of the universe . . . . God is also good. He made the earth for his glory and in the end restores it to its former glory, indeed, to a glory it never dreamed of having. God's goodness extends to the believers in guiding and protecting them from eternal harm and to evildoers in calling them to repentance.'

What does Revelation mean?

Dennis Bratcher in his article 'Interpreting the Book of Revelation,' 'A text cannot mean what it never could have meant to its original authors or hearers.'

Bratcher: 'There are several distinct features of apocalyptic writing:

-It arises out of historical context of great turmoil, persecution, and oppression.
-It is carefully crafted literature.
-It is presented in the form of visions, dreams, and other worldly journeys.
-Its images and symbols are form of fantasy rather than reality, and its language is cryptic, metaphorical, and highly symbolic.'

The author of Revelations knew his Hebrew Scriptures inside and out. There are hundreds of references to Old Testament scripture in the book.

Bratcher provides a couple of hints for when we read Revelation. 'The rich and varied cultural context of the ancient world must be the frame of reference for interpreting the names and symbols of the book, but also with a sensitivity to how creatively they are used in the book. The visions and symbols should not be pressed into allegory in which every detail has some meaning: most often the meaning is in the entire vision and its impact rather than every detail.'

'Blessed is the one who reads aloud the words of the prophecy, and blessed are those who hear and who keep what is written in it; for the time is near. John to the seven churches that are in Asia . . . To him who loves us and freed us from our sins by his blood, and made us to be a kingdom of priests serving his God and Father, to him be glory and dominion forever and ever . . . Look, his is coming with the clouds; and every eye will see him . . . So it is to be. Amen.' Revelation 1:3-7

John had visions and was commissioned to write about them. He saw the very throne of God.

"When I saw him, I fell at his feet as though dead. But he placed his right hand on me, saying, 'Do not be afraid; I am the first and the last, and the living one. I was dead, and see, I am alive, forever and ever, and I have the keys of Death and of Hades.' Revelation 1:17-18

'The seven lampstands are the seven churches.' Revelation 1:20

John then had a word to each of the churches. Sometimes he was encouraging and sometimes he was correcting.

'To the church in Ephesus . . . I know that you are enduring patiently and bearing up for the sake of my name . . . But I have this against you, that you have abandoned the love you had at first . . . . I will come and remove your lampstand from its place unless you repent . . . . To everyone who conquers, I will give permission to eat from the tree of life that is in the paradise of God. Revelation 2:3-7

'To the church in Laodicea . . . I know your works; you are neither cold nor hot. I wish that you were either cold or hot. So, because you are lukewarm, and neither cold nor hot, I am about to spit you out of my mouth.' Revelation 3:14-16

'Listen! I am standing at the door; if you hear my voice and open the door, I will come in and eat with you, and you with me . . . . let anyone who has an ear listen to what the Spirit is saying to the churches.' Revelation 3; 20, 22

Chapters 4-22 describe John's vision in very graphic imagery. There are beasts, horseman, and all kinds of other exotic creatures.

Richard and Julia Wilke in their Disciple handbook write about the meaning of these visions that the churches in Asia who were under intense persecution from Rome would have gleaned from the writing:

'Trouble is coming. Be sure which side you are one. The four horseman- conquest, war famine, and death- are coming . . . . You are either in or out, washed in the blood of the Lamb or doomed, wearing either the mark of the Lamb or the mark of the beast.

Fallen, fallen is Babylon the great! (18:2) . . . Stand firm. The day will soon come when the Roman Empire, awful whore, slayer of God's people, will be gone from the face of the earth.

Evil will be destroyed once and for all. Christ is married to his bride, his holy people (Revelation 19:7). Satan first will be bound (20:2) and then finally thrown into a lake of fire. (20:10) Even death itself shall die (2-:14) and God will bring a new heaven and a new earth.'

'And the four living creatures, each of them with six wings, are full of eyes all around, and inside. Day and night without ceasing they sing,

Holy, holy, holy,
The Lord God Almighty,
Who was and is and is to come.' Revelation 4:8

Scrolls, horses, sadness and devastation.

'And out come another horse, bright red; its rider was permitted to take peace from the earth, so that people would slaughter one another.' Revelation 6:4

Dragons and angels.

'And war broke out in heaven; Michael and his angels fought against the dragon. 'Revelation 12:7

Rome is going down. 'Fallen, fallen is Babylon the great! Revelation 14:7

'After this, I heard what seemed to be the loud voice of a great multitude in heaven, saying,

'Hallelujah!

Salvation and glory and power to our God,
For his judgments are true and just.' Revelation 19:1-2

'Then I saw the thrones, and those seated on them were given authority to judge, I also saw the souls of those who had been beheaded for their testimony to Jesus and for the word of God. They had not worshipped the beast or its image and had not received its mark on their foreheads or their hands. They came to life and reigned with Christ a thousand years.' Revelation 20:4

'Then I saw a new heaven and a new earth . . . He will dwell with them; they will be his peoples . . . he will wipe every tear from their eyes. Death will be no more; mourning and crying and paid will be no more, for the first things have passed away.'
Revelation 21:1, 3-4

'See, I am coming soon, my reward is with me, to repay according to everyone's work. I am the Alpha and the Omega, the first and the last, the beginning and the end . . . . Let everyone who is thirsty come. Let anyone who wishes take the water of life as a gift . . . . Amen. Come, Lord Jesus!' Revelation 22:12, 17, 20

There are lots of approaches to interpreting the book of Revelation, none of them sufficient in themselves. There are lots of concepts in the Bible on which we might dwell other than God; Satan, angels, demons, end times, or the second coming of Christ as examples. We will not be rewarded by dismissing or placing too much emphasis on any one of these.

Baker Commentary: 'This is perhaps a good note on which to end, for all the views agree that when historical time ends, we shall be forever with the Lord. With that ultimate prospect before us, let us be content.'

This concludes my posts of the Bible in one year. Happy faith trails!

References

Asa, Robert, *The Faith of a Skeptic: The Enigma of Ecclesiastes*, Journal for the Liberal Arts and Sciences, Summer 2009

Barth, Karl, *Epistle to the Philippians, 40th Anniversary Edition*, Westminster John Knox Press, 2002

Bartlett, David, *Romans, Westminster Bible Companion*, Westminster John Knox Press, 1995

Blair Vs Hitchens – Full Transcript (Munk Debate, Religion), November 2010, http://keeptonyblairforpm.wordpress.com/2010/11/28/blair-vs-hitchens-full-transcript-munk-debate-religion/

Bratcher, Dennis, Interrupting the Book of Revelation, 2009, http://www.crivoice.org/therevelation.html

Brueggemann, Walter *Praying the Psalms*, Saint Mary's Press, 1982

Brueggemann, Walter, *Theology of the Old Testament, Testimony, Dispute, Advocacy* Augsburg, Fortress, 1992

Charles, Larry, Seinfeld, Episode '*The Statue*', http://www.seinfeldscripts.com/TheStatue.htm

Christmas Songs 2, *Sweet Little Jesus Boy*, http://www.cowboylyrics.com/lyrics/christmas-songs-2/sweet-little-jesus-boy-14434.html

Collins, Phil, *Another Day in Paradise*, http://www.lyricsfreak.com/p/phil+collins/another+day+in+paradise_20108035.html

Craddock, Fred, *1 and 2 Peter and Jude*, Westminster Bible Companion, Westminster John Knox Press, 1995

Davis, Ellen, *Proverbs, Ecclesiastes, and the Song of Songs*, Westminster Bible Companion, Westminster John Knox Press, 2000

Donelson, Lewis, *Colossians, Ephesians, 1 and 2 Timothy*, Westminster Bible Companion, Westminster John Knox Press, 1996

Elwell, Walter, eds, *Baker Commentary on the Bible*, Baker Books, 1989

Fairchild, Mary, *Book of Leviticus, Introduction to the Book of Leviticus*, http://christianity.about.com/od/oldtestamentbooks/qt/leviticusintro.htm

Fretheim, Terence E, *1 and 2 Kings*, Westminster Bible Companion, Westminster John Knox Press, 1999

Grench, Frances Taylor, *Hebrews and James*, Westminster Bible Companion, Westminster John Knox Press, 1996

Gumbel, Nicky, *Alpha - Questions of Life*, An Opportunity to Explore the Questions of Life, Alpha North America, 2007

Hahn, Roger, *The Book of Job - Introduction*, http://www.crivoice.org/Biblestudy/bbjob1.html

Heschel, Abraham Joshua, *Moral Audacity and Spiritual Grandeur*, Farrar, Straus, Giroux, 1997

Heschel, Abraham Joshua, *The Prophets*, Harper and Row, 1962

Howell, James, *Exploring Christianity, The Bible, Faith, and Life*, Trinity Press International, 2001

Howell, James, eYear Through The Bible, http://www.mpumc.org/sermons-and-writings/dr-howells-eseries.cfm/series/2C3ED3D9-19B9-E193-F4236B0E00CA8F29

Jacobs, Louis Rabbi, *Song of Songs*, http://www.myjewishlearning.com/texts/Bible/Writings/Song_of_Songs.shtml

Janzen, Gerald J., *Exodus, Westminster Bible Companion*, Westminster John Knox Press, 1997

Kalas, Ellsworth J., *A Hop, Skip, and a Jump through the Bible*, Abington Press, 2007

Kracker, Uncle, *Good to be me*, http://www.metrolyrics.com/good-to-be-me-lyrics-uncle-kracker.html

Lisher Richard, *The Interrupted Sermon, 1996*,

Long, Thomas, *Matthew, Westminster Bible Companion*, Westminster John Knox Press, 1997

Murphy, Roland E., *The Gift of the Psalms*, Hendrickson Publishers, Inc, 2000

Murphy, Roland E., *The Tree of Life, An Exploration of Biblical Wisdom Literature*, William B. Eerdmans, Publishing Company, 2002

Paul II, John, *Rise, Let Us Be On Our Way*, Warner Books, 2004

Peterson, Eugene H., *1 and 2 Samuel, Westminster Bible Companiony*, Westminster John Knox Press, 1999

Pressler Carolyn, *Joshua, Judges, and Ruth, Westminster Bible Companion*, Westminster John Knox Press, 2002.

Ringe, Sharon, Luke, Westminster Bible Companion, Westrminster John Knox Press, 1995

Roberts, Mark, *Can we Trust the Gospels*, Crossway Books, 2007

Sestieri, Lea, *Term 'Spirit' Translates the Hebrew Word ruah*, http://www.adishakti.org/_/term_spirit_translates_the_hebrew.htm

Spurgeon, Charles, *Mornings and Evenings*, Hendrickson Publishers, 1995

Sugarland, *You might just make me believe*, http://www.azlyrics.com/lyrics/sugarland/justmightmakemebelieve.html

Sutherland, Robert, *The Biblical Book of Job, A literary, legal and philosophical study*, www.bookofjob.org

The Catholic Encyclopedia, http://www.newadvent.org/cathen/

The Jewish Study Bible, Tanakh Translation, Oxford University Press, 2004

The New Interpreter's Study Bible, NRSV with the Apocrypha, Abington Press, 2003

The Oxford Bible Commentary, (eds Barton and Muddiman), Oxford University Press, 2001

Vistotzky, Burton L. *Reading the Book*, Making the Bible a Timeless Text, First JPS edition, 2005

Walasky, Paul, *Acts, Westminster Bible Companion*, 1998

Weir, Bill, '*Exclusive: Rescued Miner Says Experience Renewed His Faith in God*', http://abcnews.go.com/International/exclusive-rescued-miner-ricardo-villaroel-experience-renewed-faith/story?id=11876860

Westermann, Claus *Genesis, An Introduction*, Augsburg Fortress, 1992

Wright, N. T., *Simply Christian, Why Christianity Makes Sense*, Harper One, 2006

BIO

I was born in Marietta, Georgia in 1961. I am currently employed with RaceTrac Petroleum. I have been married for 20 years. My wife works in the medical field for Children's Hospital in Atlanta. I also have two children. The oldest is a rising sophomore at Georgia Southern University. The youngest is a club soccer player and will be a freshman in high school this fall. I enjoy reading, studying and teaching the Bible. In my spare time, I enjoy photography and landscaping.

Since my mid thirties, I have been serious about my Christian faith. A dozen years ago, I had the privilege of having Dr. James Howell as my Senior Pastor while attending his church in North Carolina. It was Dr. Howell's presentation of the Bible, his intellectual style of speaking and writing that prompted me to become more attentive to my faith. For the last decade, I have immersed myself in serious study of the Bible and have read a wide variety of serious religious literature.

I am currently a lay teacher at Douglasville First United Methodist Church in Douglasville, Georgia. I teach several adult Bible study classes including 'The Alpha Course.'

CPSIA information can be obtained at www.ICGtesting.com
Printed in the USA
LVOW100017131211

259066LV00001B/126/P